A PERSONAL JOURNEY TO THE
HEART OF TEACHING

JOHN FIORAVANTI

ICEBERG

Published in Canada by Iceberg Publishing, Waterloo

Library and Archives Canada Cataloguing in Publication
Fioravanti, John, 1951-
     A personal journey to the heart of teaching / John
Fioravanti.
ISBN 978-0-9780916-5-1
     1. Fioravanti, John, 1951-. 2. Teachers--Canada--
Biography.
I. Title.

LA2325.F55A3 2007   370.92   C2007-902359-2

Distributed by:
Iceberg Publishing
55 Northfield Drive East, Suite 171
Waterloo ON N2K 3T6
Tel: 519.572.1479 Fax: 519.747.7763
contact@icebergpublishing.com
www.icebergpublishing.com

First paperback printing: May 2007
Second paperback printing: August 2008
Photos by: Kenneth Tam

Printed in Canada by Friesens, Altona, MB.

A PERSONAL JOURNEY TO THE
HEART OF TEACHING

JOHN FIORAVANTI

CAUSATION - W.W. I.
pride - to be #1
competition - tensions
Imperialism
equipment + all armed forces
added tensions
Security in numbers

Dedications

For Anne, my bride of thirty-three years… because you are always by my side and teach me to love unconditionally.

For Dianna, my daughter… because in your eyes I am ten feet tall even when I feel much smaller.

For my sons, Dan and Dominic… because you challenge me to be the best father I can be.

For Kenneth, my dear friend… because you believed in me and gave me the quiet, encouraging command that made this book possible —"Engage!"

For all my friends and colleagues… because you carried me when I stumbled in doubt.

Introduction

When I was asked to write a book about teaching, I was both surprised and humbled. The surprise had its roots in the fact that I have never viewed myself as a 'master teacher'. I felt humbled because I was being given a great honour.

As I quietly speculated upon the likely contents of such a work, it became apparent that it could not be a technical manual filled with practical aids teachers could utilize in their planning, the execution of their lessons, and the evaluation and reporting processes. That possibility left me cold, despite the importance of these things to all teachers.

One might say I am an incurable romantic in that

my emotions have a lot to do with who I am, what I do, and why I do things. I must write about that which inspires passion within me. I am driven also by a desire to share. Therefore, this book is about my passionate journey through a wonderful career in a sacred profession. My years in the classroom have been, and still are, wonderful — full of wonder — because of the young women and men who teach me so much. Often, I have quipped to others that my students have taught me more than I have taught them. As I reflect on that remark, tossed out so lightly, it has more truth than one might suppose. The teaching profession is 'sacred' because parents entrust their most precious treasures to my care. The responsibility is both exhilarating and humbling at the same time.

My hope, as I recount my personal journey through these years of growth, is to illuminate somewhat the path a young teacher travels upon towards achieving the expectations that this profession imposes. These expectations of excellence are ideals. They are inspiring and frightening at the same time. In my case, the fear was debilitating, and it came close to terminating my quest for excellence in my profession. I know that this circumstance has been, and is, shared by many other young teachers. Hopefully, this labour of love will provide solace, a sense of camaraderie, and inspiration to focus on the real 'heart' of teaching.

CHAPTER I
A Small Town Kid

B eing a teenager in the 1960s was a pretty heady experience as I look back on it. The period was fraught with change: the advent of rock 'n roll music, the anti-war protests, the anti-Establishment attitudes, the sexual revolution, and the rebirth of the women's movement. As I consider it all, the best way to describe the period is as an age of idealism. I remember quite clearly my own personal struggle to remain apart, or rather, to be unique among my peers. I recall the contempt I felt for the many teens who seemed compelled to copy the Beatle hair styles and then the longer, shaggier fashions which followed and endured into the 1970s. Some felt the need to express their rebellion through their clothing; some played with drugs; and others indulged in sexual experimentation. As many of my peers were determined to conform to the newly emerging teen sub-culture, I found myself alienated from its outward manifestations. I felt driven to be apart from these superficialities and experimentations, but not isolated from my teen contemporaries. Although I didn't realize it at the time, this need to be my own person would loom large in my adult years.

If the behaviour of many teens turned me off, the idealism of that period had a significant and life-long effect on my personal philosophy. What emerged as an important principle in my life was the belief that people, as unique human beings, are more important than groups, organizations, institutions, or the quest for wealth. The seeds of this conviction first emerged when, as a child in elementary school, I felt at odds with my own desire to belong to a group of friends and the guilt experienced when someone else was excluded. Later, as I contemplated entry into the seminary to study for the Roman Catholic priesthood, I discovered that the Church insisted on strict conformity and the sacrifice of personal preferences. I remember meeting with my parish pastor to discuss the interview I was scheduled to have with the bishop. He told me that I must remove my long sideburns before the interview. Seeing my reluctance, he insisted that the bishop would dismiss my application out of hand when he saw my facial hair. The following week I saw my pastor after Mass to tell him the interview had gone very well and I had been accepted. When he noticed I still had my sideburns, he told me that I would not last long in the seminary because I had failed my first test — that of obedience. I had failed to conform. Inwardly I rejoiced — I had determined in my own mind that the well-being of the individual was paramount. Ironically, while this belief was taking root within me, it did not bring me to be sympathetic to the women's movement

— that would come later.

I feel very fortunate to have grown up in Dundas, Ontario. This small town of just 5,000 people when we arrived in 1955 would grow to over 20,000 people by the time I moved out in 1973. It was a quiet town nestled beside Hamilton's west end, and just one hour southeast of Toronto, my birthplace. At that time Hamilton, on Lake Ontario, boasted just over 300,000 people, was home to McMaster University, three hospitals, and ample shopping outlets. It was Canada's steel city and when the wind blew the wrong way, it shared its air pollution with Dundas. As a youngster, I didn't have to leave Dundas in order to play organized sports, but I did have to travel by city bus to Hamilton to attend my Catholic high school. Dundas had the wholesomeness of a small town, while nearby Hamilton had the exciting big city attractions.

My pre-teen and teen years were full of activity as I played hockey in the Dundas Police Minor League and distinguished myself as a good defenseman. I idolized Tim Horton of my beloved Maple Leafs and had many opportunities to watch him play in Maple Leaf Gardens because an uncle had turned over his two season tickets to my father. My older brother Peter, our younger brother Patrick and I took turns going to the games with dad. It was my good fortune to be in the Gardens the night the Leafs clinched their last Stanley Cup of the twentieth century in 1967. I had screamed myself so hoarse I could not talk in a clear voice for days afterward.

I loved to hang out with my friends, tobogganing and ice skating on our own backyard rinks or at the Dundas Arena. In the summer I played baseball and by Little League I had become a pitcher and third baseman. In the sports of hockey and baseball, I felt a need to excel. As a Little League pitcher, I accomplished the very elusive goal of pitching a no-hitter. As a hockey defenseman, I was invited to try out for the Hamilton Junior B Red Wings, but I declined as I believed my high school studies would suffer.

My free time with my buddies became limited when my dad hired me at his I.G.A. grocery store as a part-time worker during the summer months. I was just twelve and under age, but no one questioned it as I looked older than I was. Once I reached high school I worked the year round. As the second son working in the store, following my brother Peter, I was gradually trained to work in all of the departments. I was trained in the meat department to take over when our meat manager went on vacation. I worked as a cashier and even helped my mother from time to time with the office work. Although my siblings and I were not paid any differently from the other part-time employees, there were greater expectations placed upon us as family of the owner. Dad took very little time off as owner and manager of this thriving business, and he expected the same of us. This became a sore point as social activities had to be missed during my high school years. I became resentful of the family business and my negative attitude would drive a wedge between myself and my family during my university years.

As I reflect on my high school years, my easiest relationships were with my close friends as we shared so many things in common. In those days, during the mid to late 1960s, one of the best places for us to meet girls was at a CYO dance. Most local parishes had a Catholic Youth Organization, and St. Augustine's in Dundas was no exception. However, each month St. Joe's parish in Hamilton had what was called a district dance. Now those were quite large, the bands were great, and the girls plentiful! I remember how much I wanted a steady girlfriend throughout those years, but my mother had a rule: no steady girlfriend until I was eighteen. Unfortunately for me, my eighteenth birthday wouldn't arrive until January of my last year in high school. So I dated several different girls and fell in love on more than one occasion… at least I thought it was love! It seemed that I was forever focusing my attention on the wrong girl. That didn't do my self-confidence a lot of good, but it didn't shatter me either.

My mother made a comment to me once that I will always treasure. She told me that she liked it when my friends came over to our house. She said I had very good taste in friends. I still do.

My toughest relationships were with my parents — after I started working at the store. The lines became blurred between our relationship at home and our employer-employee relationship at work. I had a lot of trouble with that. It seemed to me that my parents valued the other part-time employees (many of whom were friends of myself and Peter) more than me. I remember feeling resentful and that led to a negative attitude on the job. My family members were not great communicators, so I didn't learn to sit down and thrash out issues that upset me. Instead they festered as I opted to keep them to myself, or to share with a few close friends. I never felt unloved, just very dissatisfied with my life. I admired my parents who were tireless workers and did their best to teach my siblings and me good values. They made it clear that the four of us (we had a sister, Mary Jane, five years my junior and third born) were capable of a university education and they expected us to get our degrees. I respected and loved my parents, but I did not feel close to them. So my feelings of alienation revolved around the store, and that reality would loom large as I made decisions about university.

CHAPTER 2
Snow Shovels and a Phone Booth

While I was navigating my way through those tumultuous young years, and feeling more and more isolated from my family, I was also becoming aware of a compulsion developing within me. I *needed* to help people. At the time, I didn't really understand why, but I came to realize that helping others gave me a tremendous sense of fulfillment — it made me feel as if powerful floodlights had switched on within me. As my parents seemed to grow distant from me, it was this need that began to influence me when it came time to choose a path for my career. It just took me a while to realize what the need really was, and what path I could follow to satisfy it.

In the beginning, my need manifested itself in simple ways. One incident which comes to mind occurred after a severe winter storm. I was about ten years old, and I remember donning my boots, coat, hat and scarf, grabbing the big scoop shovel, crossing the street and shoveling out a few of the neighbours' driveways. One sweet elderly lady came outside to offer me money. I politely refused and continued my work. Then she offered me hot chocolate and cookies when I was finished. I declined once more because I didn't want her to think I expected a reward. Her surprise and delight had been my prize, and I loved it — I felt appreciated. Now I regret I didn't accept her second offer, as I had denied myself the opportunity to get to know her a bit. My dad wasn't too impressed — he wanted to know why our driveway wasn't cleared out yet! I didn't have a good answer for him.

Another incident occurred on a nice spring

Sunday morning, two years later. We had just pulled into the driveway after church and were exiting the car when dad accused me of not washing the car the day before. I had washed the car and was stung by his accusation. The ensuing shouting match ended when dad threatened to turn me out onto the streets. I stomped off in my good suit, saying I wouldn't be back. My Irish temper (inherited from my mother) got me into trouble quite frequently. So, I walked downtown and soon found myself back at the church. What was I going to do now? I didn't even have any money. Muttering to myself, I went inside, and slid into a back pew to think. Unknown to me, my mother had chased my dad out to look for me, but he never figured I'd be back inside the church.

Despite the soothing sounds of the liturgical music, I didn't cool off. I didn't pray much either. But I did make a decision — to hitchhike my way to Toronto where my paternal grandparents lived. I wasn't worried about doing that because, again, I was big for my age and people told me I looked a few years older than I actually was. Besides, I was still angry, so heaven help anyone who tried to mess with me. Luckily it took just two rides with nice older gentlemen to get me within a few blocks of my grandparents' street in Toronto, an hour away from my home in Dundas.

As I walked briskly towards my destination, I came upon a scene at an old style telephone booth — the kind Superman liked to use. Inside was a small boy who looked to be about five years old, and outside, pounding on the door, was his very distraught mother. At first I thought the kid was playing a game and his mother was having none of it. As I drew close, I could see the woman was frightened, not angry, and the little boy was in tears as he pounded on the inside of the door.

"Do you need any help, ma'am?" I asked.

"Please! The door! Help me get my boy out!" she pleaded as she stepped aside for me. I could see that the door folded inwards at the centre, so I pointed to the side of the booth where I wanted the boy to stand. Surprisingly, the door opened without much trouble and the boy bolted outside and into the arms of his mother.

"Oh thank you, thank you, thank you!" she cried through her tears. "You are a hero!" she declared as she hugged the boy tightly to herself.

Totally embarrassed, I wished them well and continued on my way. A hero? Me? No way! As I mentally ticked off all the deficiencies that disqualified me as a hero, I suddenly realized how wonderful and warm I felt. In that instant, all the morning's troubles and anger fell away like sheets of ice in the face of a quick thaw. Maybe I was a worthwhile person after all. As I sauntered on my way, with a quickening step, I was glowing inside. That was when I really began to realize that I loved to help people. The only question left was how. Lucky for me, the answer would only take a few more years, and a few more clues, to unravel.

◆◆◆

I was in high school when I discovered that I possessed two key abilities I thought would make me a good classroom teacher. One day at home, I walked into the dining room to ask my mother something. She was sitting at one end of the table doing some paperwork for my dad's business. My little sister was at the other end of the table doing homework. Before I could say anything, my mother looked up at me, heaved one of her famous Irish sighs, and asked me to help my visibly upset sister. As I plunked myself down in a chair beside her, I asked, "Hey M.J., whatcha got here?"

"Stupid old math!" she retorted in disgust.

"Here, let me take a look," I said as I slid her textbook in front of me. After reading the problem, I slid the book back to her and proceeded to ask her a series of questions about the problem, the answers to which led her to the correct solution and to an insight as to how to tackle these kinds of problems. Smiling, M.J. thanked me and turned back to her homework.

As I rose from the chair, my mother said quietly, "John, you're a natural born teacher, you know."

No, I didn't know that, but I thought about it a lot in the years to come. As other incidents occurred later, confirming this ability, I gradually became aware that I could break down complex things and explain them to others. Where did this ability come from? Did I learn it by osmosis from someone else? Or was I born with it as my mother believed? I couldn't answer those questions, but I felt grateful for the gift — it gave me another way to help.

In addition to this mysterious ability, I discovered that I could perform for an audience. While in grade ten, I joined the parish CYO which was forming a drama group to compete in a Hamilton festival featuring one act plays. Our director, from the local little theatre group, decided to cast me as the male lead playing opposite a very lovely grade thirteen student as her fiancé. I thought I had died and gone to heaven. I warned the director that I had never acted and I was three years younger than the female lead. He just laughed and said to me quietly behind his hand, "Don't worry son, you look older and I'm sure you can act."

How could he know that? I didn't know that! But I didn't argue with him too strenuously — after all, this part would give me the opportunity to work very closely with a gorgeous young lady. I just looked up to heaven and quietly gave thanks.

Yes, I fell in love with her, and of course, nothing came of it.

Two months later the big night arrived and we prepared to perform on the festival stage. The set was ready, as were the props. The curtain went up and we began to perform. All went well until it came time for me to switch on a lamp and tell the rest of the cast a ghost story. The stage lights went out; I switched on the lamp, and… nothing. Nothing! Not sure what to do in the total darkness, I started talking to the other characters beside me about stupid lamps that don't work — and that went on for about two very long minutes. The lamp suddenly came alive; I thanked the gods, and continued with my ghost story. Afterward, the adjudicator praised our performance and said he was impressed by the inspired ad-libbing by George, the lead character, when the lamp didn't go on.

"That was very quick thinking, George, and very effective!"

Our director, sitting beside me, elbowed me in the ribs, and said, "Told ya so!" I guess he had. All I knew was that I was really excited while onstage and disappointed that it was all over.

Two years later, I was offered the chance to perform again, but in a different way, and in front of a different kind of audience. I joined a group of students from four other local Catholic high schools to raise awareness of the value of Catholic education to the community, and we were tasked with public speaking engagements before student assemblies at all five of our area's Catholic high schools. Knowing about my involvement with the group, my pastor surprised me one Sunday morning by asking me to give my talk at Mass — as a guest homilist. The talks went well despite my nervousness, but what surprised me somewhat was the discovery that I really enjoyed the experience. So now I knew I could speak well in front of an audience as well as act.

By the time I was a senior high school student, I had reflected on all these experiences enough to realize I had some abilities that would work well in a teaching career. It wasn't just a logical decision, though: my years at Cathedral High in Hamilton had cultivated a deep respect for the teachers there and I felt a growing desire to emulate my favourites among them. They had helped me to be successful in my studies, but more importantly, they made me feel good just to be me. I had always viewed myself with a jaded eye — I was my own worst enemy in that regard. These men taught me to look at myself and others with a more balanced eye. They even taught me to laugh at myself. Not only was I grateful, but I wanted to be just like them.

As I went off to St. Jerome's College at the University of Waterloo, I knew in my heart that I wanted a career in teaching. I was convinced that it would satisfy my need to help. Emerging from the inner wars and struggles of my teen years, I also knew I wanted to help teens — maybe I could help them avoid some of the mistakes I had made. It was very clear to me that I hadn't handled personal issues within my family well at all. Too often, I gave my Irish temper full rein and thus made difficult situations far worse than need be. I felt I had abilities that would fit the world of teaching as well. I could easily recognize the nature of an academic problem, and come up with questions that led others, step by step, to an understanding that had eluded them. I knew I wanted to do something special — to make a difference.

CHAPTER 3
Meeting my Demon

When I began my university studies in 1969, I had two clear goals in mind. First, I wanted to determine whether or not I had a vocation to the Catholic priesthood; and second, I wanted to become a teacher. Since many of my high school teachers were priests who worked in parishes in the evenings and on weekends, I was hopeful that I too could combine these two professions. In those days, a person wanting to teach in the elementary grades (Kindergarten through grade ten) was obliged to get their university degree first, and then apply to an elementary teacher's college. Those who wished to teach high school (grades nine through thirteen) applied to a secondary teacher's college after obtaining their degree. My plan to combine the careers of teaching and the priesthood meant that I would live in a seminary residence while I pursued my university degree. The Church called this period of undergraduate studies the 'Philosophy years', because seminarians were expected to major in Philosophy and Religious Studies. The 'Theology years' would follow graduation from my bachelor's degree — four years of theological studies and training for the priesthood. In my interview with the Bishop of Hamilton, I had received permission to pursue studies in History as a double major during my Philosophy years.

This decision to pursue my university studies in a seminary bewildered both my friends and my family. Everyone knew I wanted to be married and to have my own family some day, so what had gotten into me? For a decade prior to my decision, I had served as an altar boy in my home parish. That experience, which I had enjoyed immensely, combined with the overt suggestions by the nuns who taught me in the elementary school in Dundas, and the priests who taught at my high school, had planted within me a suspicion that I might have a 'calling' to the priesthood. Then, early in my grade thirteen year, I had a personal crisis after having two accidents with my parents' cars — within weeks of each other. I was so overcome with guilt and anxiety, that in desperation I turned to prayer. In a short time the crisis passed and I felt at peace within myself. I took that to be a real sign.

Any attempts to explain why I felt I might have a call to the priesthood did nothing to diminish the skepticism that surrounded me. I discovered later that my family had theorized my decision, which required I go away from home, was just a creative way around my parents' mandate that my siblings and I all go to university in Hamilton, and remain at home to help out in the family business. Because of these doubts, I left home to embark on my new adventure with grave self-doubts, the mirthful skepticism of my friends, and disapproval from my family. There was nothing malicious in any of the reactions of family or friends, but it was hurtful that they didn't believe me. If that wasn't upsetting enough, I was scared silly of being away from home and adopting a celibate lifestyle. By the time I reached the seminary, I had lost any self-confidence I'd managed to develop over the years. I had serious doubts, but I had to put the nagging question about a calling to rest — one way or the other.

Throughout the eighteen months spent in the seminary, I made a few life-long friends among my fellow seminarians who helped me further develop the habit of introspection. In a sense, they became my new family. I felt estranged from my own family and the high school friends who were afraid to talk or joke about certain subjects since I was studying to be a priest. Many of my fellow seminarians were like brothers to me as they helped me to grow personally during that time. One in particular, John Koester from Baltimore, Maryland, became a life-long friend. His early years, though different than mine, provided us with a lot of common ground. John is a deep thinker and is profoundly spiritual. He searched for meaning in his studies and in his daily living, and in doing so, he inspired me to do the same. We would meet daily in his room or mine for coffee (always coffee!) and serious conversation about world issues, family relationships, and events occurring on campus at the University of Waterloo and in the seminary. Almost every evening we would walk together around the oval driveway that surrounded the two seminary buildings. Although we interacted with the other students at the university, we didn't identify with them. We were so serious about our lives — our studies and our future — while the other students seemed to be driven by different things, like where the next party would occur.

There were many instances where we would sit with other students to talk between classes, or do the same in groups. We discovered that many of the females actually sought out the company of seminarians because we were 'safe' — we wouldn't be asking them out on dates. They could talk more freely with us about things that were important to them, without having to worry about impressing us as potential suitors. We suspected, too, that some of them saw us as a challenge to their feminine charms, and were actually trying to get us to date them and to leave the seminary, and that did happen to a few seminarians. Those friendly situations caused me a great deal of trouble, especially when I found myself in the company of a young woman who was very attractive. And I'll be honest, the sky-high mini skirts that were fashionable in 1969 did not help me one little bit! But these were frustrating challenges that we seminarians had in common and shared. As I struggled with the issue of celibacy, I became increasingly frustrated and unhappy. Some seminarians were able to cope with this challenge, and continued their studies through to ordination. After a year and a half, I decided that God would have little use for a profoundly unhappy celibate. I acted on that decision, and completed my History degree as a non-religious student. Facing these challenges taught me how to share things that bothered me. I learned some difficult lessons that I have cherished my whole life, like the need to be generous and compassionate, to respect others as unique individuals, and to be slow to judge. Deciding to leave that seminarian family was one of the most difficult things I have had to do in my life, but it had to be done.

As I packed my belongings to go home for Christmas in December of 1970, I was an emotional mess. The assistant pastor in my home parish had been very supportive when I decided to enter the seminary, and he remained so throughout much of my adult life. When I told him I had decided to leave the seminary, he put his finger on the resulting internal chaos I was experiencing. He said that I probably felt a great sense of failure. It was true. I had a profound sense of personal failure. I knew I wasn't a bad person, but I didn't feel very positive about myself either. Not only did I feel that I had failed those who supported my entry into the seminary, but I felt that the estrangement from my family and friends had been for naught.

Shortly thereafter, one of my old high school buddies elbowed me gently in the ribs, winked, and said that mothers and fathers had better lock up their daughters real quick! I laughed with him, but I was crying on the inside. Who would want me, I asked myself. I would never admit it to my friends at home, but I knew I could not ask any girl out on a date. I believed that a rejection would destroy me. I was too consumed with personal failure to give the possibility any serious thought.

As I prepared to return to Waterloo for the new term in January of 1971, I found myself in a new battle with my parents. They expected me to transfer back home to the local university to complete my degree now that I had given up my seminary studies. I refused. It wasn't rebellion, it was terror. I had to return to Waterloo, to the only place on the planet where I felt comfortable. I knew the school, I respected the professors, my seminary friends were studying there, and I loved the city. Of course, this just confirmed my family's earlier beliefs about my motives: I was still running away from home, and from my father's store. The irony is they had that backwards: I was running *to* what I perceived as home. In order to get approval to go back to Waterloo, I had to reach a compromise with my father, requiring me to return home every weekend on the bus to work at our family store. It was not an ideal solution for me, but I hoped it would mend fences with my family, and give me the opportunity to see more of my old friends. It didn't work on either count.

When I returned to Waterloo after Christmas that year, I was determined to finish my History degree and then apply to a teacher's college. The sense of failure at having left the seminary still plagued me, but I hoped I could overcome it and become a teacher. I also knew I wanted to find the right girl to marry. Did I deliberately put myself in the company of girls on campus, or ask any of them out? No, I was in hiding — emotionally. I felt whipped. I felt unworthy. Had I left the Church in bitterness when I left the seminary? No, I was more prayerful than ever. I needed serious fixing — I needed a miracle, but I didn't ask for one. I didn't believe that I deserved one. I got one anyway.

Because of the family compromise that made it necessary to bus home each Friday afternoon, I changed my Saturday morning Philosophy class to another offered on Wednesday evenings. That upset me because some of my brothers from the seminary were taking the Saturday class. Nevertheless, I had to abide by our agreement, so I made the change.

As I entered the classroom that first Wednesday evening in January, I noticed that a beautiful young lady named Anne Runstedler was already in the room, waiting for class to start. We had met in first year when we took the same introductory English and Philosophy courses. I remember that she had taken pity on me when I couldn't borrow a typewriter to finish a Philosophy paper, and offered to type it for me. Seeing her again that Wednesday evening, I found myself wishing I had the nerve to ask her out. I laughed disgustedly at myself, thinking that a wonderful girl like Anne could do much better. What would she want with a depressed, mixed up loser like me? Then I remembered that the year before, she'd had a boyfriend, so there was no point in daydreaming about impossible scenarios. I didn't want to risk a rejection that would prove I was a loser.

I did *not* know that Anne had broken up with her boyfriend, or that she knew I had left the seminary. I drove the torturously hopeful thoughts about her from my mind and focused on the lecture.

At break time I sat at a table by myself with my

coffee, and was very surprised when Anne asked to join me. Good grief, what would I say? I didn't have to decide, because this young woman had already determined how the conversation was going to go. I realized she knew I'd left the seminary because she asked me how I was coping with the change. But answering that question posed a problem. I wanted to lie. I wanted her to see me as a guy who had his life all together. Instead I told her that I was ok, but the transition wasn't easy. She looked at me earnestly and decided not to pursue the topic.

Then she asked if I knew about the Sadie Hawkins dance at St. Jerome's College in February — the night before I would go home for Reading Week. Embarrassed, I admitted that I didn't. She smiled and asked me if I'd be her date that night. I was in absolute shock, and I was ecstatic. I agreed enthusiastically and the two of us just sat there grinning at each other. She looked as happy as I felt. This couldn't be happening to me, but it was! Two years later we married and began a wonderful life together. Our second grandchild was born recently, and as we held that precious new life, we grinned at each other the same way we had on that night in the college cafeteria over 35 years before.

It was a blessing: I had found love and joy in my life.

My interior battles were not over, but now I was not facing those battles alone. Anne struggled to understand my insecurities and my lack of self-confidence. She couldn't, but she *could* see the man I would eventually become, and set out to make sure that I would recognize my own gifts, and to nurture my inner self. She dreamed of being a teacher too — but that hope was extinguished when, after graduation in the spring of 1972, teacher's colleges refused her applications because of her severe hearing loss. She would have to live her dream vicariously through me.

In Anne, I had the most formidable support imaginable.

♦♦♦

My professional training started in September of 1972 at Hamilton Teacher's College on the McMaster University campus, and I began it without much self-confidence. Although I really wanted to teach high school students, I decided to train at the local elementary teacher's college because I couldn't afford to go away to the secondary teacher's colleges in Toronto or London. My difficulties with my family did not improve. I didn't feel comfortable at home or in the store, so when I wasn't in Waterloo with Anne, I was out with my friends in Dundas.

Was I trying to work things out with my family? No, I was sweeping the problems under the carpet hoping they'd go away. To make matters worse, Anne felt that the family didn't like or accept her because of her severe hearing loss. It was 'us' versus 'them'. We were engaged in April of 1972, despite my mother's objections that at 21 we were too young, and the wedding date was set for the end of June 1973. The pressure was on. I was about to become a husband.

I also wanted to teach, but the taste of failure had not completely left me, so I feared I would fail in this. Moreover, I was not sure that teaching young students in elementary school would work out for me. That year of teacher training was an emotional roller coaster. On the one hand I was joyfully excited as we planned and prepared our wedding; on the other, I was juggling the pressures of my studies and practice teaching. A great fear of failure was growing daily.

In March of 1973, I was on a two-week stint as a student teacher when my parents went away on a weeklong trip and left me in charge of the store. Peter was married and was teaching in the area, while Mary Jane and Patrick were still in high school, so it was up to me to open the store in the morning, race to Cambridge to my assigned elementary school, and race home after dismissal to supervise the closing of the store. It was too much, the straw that broke the camel's back. On the second day of this manic schedule, I suffered an anxiety attack that left my stomach in knots and gave me the overwhelming feeling that my life was out of control. It seemed that the walls were closing in and the roof would collapse upon me.

I told the principal of the school and my supervising teacher that I was quitting. The principal asked me to go home and rest for a day or two and reconsider. I went to the store instead — not a good idea. Alone in the break room, I sipped some coffee while my stomach churned and my head pounded with questions for which I had no answers. How could I tell Anne? What would I do with myself? How could I get married with no job prospects? The head cashier who had worked for dad for many years came in for her coffee and noticed that I was not myself.

"John, what are you doing here? Are you ok?" she sat down beside me and put her hand on my shoulder. The dam broke. I sat there blubbering like a child, repeating over and over that I didn't know what was wrong. She was quite frightened and sent me home. I drove to Waterloo instead and brokenly tried to explain things to Anne. She didn't understand and was visibly frightened, but she stood by me and insisted that I go home and rest. This time I listened to the advice and went home and tried to rest. As I tossed and turned, and prayed, I slowly came to the realization that there was a demon inside me. I had allowed it to grow by not confronting it, and now it was eating me alive. The demon had a name familiar to us all: fear. Fear that I would let down those who were important to me, that I wasn't good enough to do what I needed to do, and that my life would be a failure.

I realized at that point that if I let that fear consume me, then all those things would come true. I had no choice but to confront it before it destroyed my dreams, and the people who loved me. But how? I couldn't fight it with my fists. Instead, I had to use my reason, and raw willpower.

Reason told me that the anxiety was not based in reality, and as I examined my life looking for tangible proof of past failures that would justify the fear, I found none. I sat on the edge of my bed, clenching and unclenching my fists in anger, thinking of the fear in Anne's eyes when I left her earlier that night.

By this time I was beginning to see the seminary issue as a very important turning point in my life, not as a failure. That rational analysis did not banish the fear — I had not yet really faced it. But I think I finally had a better understanding of the fear and was determined to do battle. It was a commitment grounded in willpower — my most potent weapon. I didn't realize it then, but my battle would continue for a long time.

Fortunately, the principal and my supervising teacher welcomed me back in a caring, non-judgmental manner. When I entered the classroom, many of my students smiled at me and said that they hoped I felt better. I stood there in front of them, trying to deal with feelings of gratitude, embarrassment, and again, of fear. Determined to silence that demon, I began the lesson with an artificially created sense of confidence.

At the end of the following week, having completed my practicum, I sat in the principal's office to discuss my evaluation. It was a good one, and it included nothing about my declared intention to quit — only that I had been sick for two days. The principal told me that he hoped I would continue to teach because he believed I belonged in the classroom. I drove home that day in a state of elation, determined to continue to march on.

As I reflected on those troubled weeks, I realized that I was a very fortunate young man to have the support that I did — from Anne and from the professionals I worked with during my practicum. This realization not only encouraged me to continue to confront and battle the fear within me, but also to help others do battle with their demons. One of the lessons I had learned from my seminary brothers is that although we are all unique beings, we all have inner demons. My experiences had given me a heightened sense of compassion towards others that made me even more determined to be a helpful and sensitive person.

The classroom would be the opportunity to use my gifts to help young people who needed understanding and support — to give to them what I had received myself. I began to see my own struggle not as a crippling defect, but rather as a strength; my personal struggles had given me the empathy and compassion to listen and to help without passing judgment. I knew I was still fragile inside, but my resolve was growing.

CHAPTER 4
Mentors All

Later that spring in 1973, I was offered a teaching contract with the Waterloo Catholic Board, which I joyfully accepted. As I publicly proclaimed my vows at our wedding ceremony in June, I privately made another promise to myself — to continue my personal and professional journey no matter what obstacles were put before me. I would not allow that niggling fear of failure to chase me out of the classroom as it almost had the year before. It would end my career and diminish me as a person if I turned and ran when the going got tough.

As I look back across more than three decades at

that twenty-two year old rookie, I shake my head in wonder. I was inexperienced, impatient, and something of a perfectionist as well. I would never be content being a good teacher or a good husband and father; I was determined to be the best. These factors, along with some emotional baggage plaguing me from my university years, made my early classroom years very challenging indeed.

My first teaching assignment was at St. Benedict Junior High in Cambridge. Just a half hour drive south of Waterloo, the school had students in grades seven to ten, and I was given grade seven English, Mathematics, and Religion classes. I was especially pleased with this assignment because my teaching certificate allowed me to teach to the end of grade ten, and this junior high school operated in the same fashion as a high school. All the students had lockers and individual timetables that had them moving to classes on a rotary system — usually taught by teachers who specialized in their subject areas. Although I was disappointed that I would not be teaching History, my major in university, I understood that rookie teachers were at the bottom of the pecking order when classes were assigned — new teachers got the assignments left after the veterans had their preferred choices. I was ok with that, but I was not comfortable teaching Math — it had been my worst subject in high school. The proverbial expression 'the blind leading the blind' came to mind immediately, and the demon within awoke. I feared I would fail my students and myself.

Fortunately, I was blessed with a wonderful Math department head, Idena Bartels, who was a gifted teacher and a caring person, nearing the end of her career. After I admitted to her that I needed help, she sat with me in the department office several times each week for the entire year, teaching me how to teach these lessons to my classes. It had been hard to admit that I needed help, but as I tried to plan lessons ahead of time, I discovered that the 'new Math' curriculum was both alien and confusing to me. I was feeling panic — so I asked for help. Idena's dedicated mentoring was invaluable, and with her assistance, I struggled through that first year utilizing everything she gave to me. The fear of failure had not been stilled by her efforts, and I found myself standing in front of my students with my stomach in knots, trying valiantly to project confidence I did not feel. It was through sheer determination that I managed to keep my demon on a tight leash.

As I dealt with my inner struggle by doggedly learning my craft from the amazing men and women on staff, I discovered I had another Achilles heel — discipline, or more accurately, the lack of it. Instead of the sweet wonderful students I had expected to be in my classes, I found myself doing battle each day with kids who just wanted to be kids.

We couldn't accomplish anything without order and discipline, and I knew that, but I was at a loss as to how to make it happen. I taught in a classroom that was one of six in a semi-open area. The noise traveled from one room to the others very easily. You can imagine the insanity that resulted when several of us were running filmstrip presentations at the same time. The filmstrip commentary was played on a separate tape player, and these tapes had loud beeps that signaled when the filmstrip should be advanced. One could never be sure whose tape was beeping, and these presentations often got fouled up under such conditions. But I digress. The point here is that it was quite apparent to my self-appointed mentor in the next classroom that I was experiencing difficulties with control. This had also been pointed out to me when I had been visited (evaluated) by my principal and the school board superintendent. When I complained to the teacher next to me about behaviour in my classes, he suggested that I might stop trying to be a buddy to my students. It dawned on me that my desire to help students had manifested itself in this 'buddy' approach which was clearly not working. I had been trying to talk to the kids as a peer, instead of acting as the adult in the classroom. Not wishing to damage what I thought was a good rapport with my students, I had refrained from enforcing a good organizational structure, and from giving them consequences for their misbehaviour. I had to switch gears, and fast, because the year was drawing to a close.

I knew I didn't want to become a drill sergeant in my classroom in order to establish good discipline, but I had to put an end to the student antics that often derailed my lessons. Fortunately, I was commuting to school each day with Margie Wittig (now Zuccala) who lived near me in Waterloo. She also taught in the open area close to my own classroom — teaching the same grade seven subjects I was teaching. Margie had no discipline problems despite the fact that she was petite in stature and a female authority figure among students who, at that time, had little respect for women. Her classroom was impeccably organized and she gladly shared her practical techniques with me.

Margie was quite talented in classroom management and had set up daily routines that gave her students good structure. When students challenged her expectations, they were given immediate and fair consequences. Her generosity and my willingness to learn changed the way I would teach for the rest of my life.

I struggled with mixed results for the balance of that year because it was very difficult to establish new routines near the end of a term. Before we went home for the summer, the principal called me into his office and gently told me that I needed to improve if I wanted to continue teaching. He then said that among the entire staff, I was his weakest link. I left his office in shock. Despite my own desire to be the best teacher, I had become this man's worst teacher. The demon within me slipped its leash and I found myself sweating bullets. How could I possibly pass my inspection next year to get a permanent contract? The principal and the superintendent would both visit my classroom (at their convenience) to see what I was up to, and I wouldn't get much notice. What could I do? I needed advice.

Mentoring of new teachers in those days happened when a rookie summoned the courage to ask for help and found a willing veteran. There was no formal mentoring program in place then (it is only now, 34 years later, that the Ontario Government is creating one). Despite my willingness to ask for help and the generosity of other teachers like Margie in my open area, I was painfully aware that I might lose it all on the inspection.

I thought all summer about how I might improve my classroom management and get my classes started on the right foot. When September came, I put new organizational structures and procedures into place, and I found myself looking at this new batch of students differently. I was determined to bend them to my will. One veteran teacher told me that his policy was never to smile in class until Christmas time. I actually tried that. I wasn't mean to the kids, just strict. There were no jokes or levity in my classroom for the first few months. I was all business as I taught my grade seven Mathematics, English, and Religion classes. I taught lessons, drilled Math and English skills orally and with worksheets, and tested my students regularly. We never departed from the lessons planned for the day. It was rigid, but I felt it was working.

One point of pride came in how I dealt with students' antics: I found myself plotting ways to stay a few steps ahead of them, lest they get out of control. I was quite good at that, but as I proudly talked about my techniques one day when Anne and I were visiting my family, my father stopped me in my tracks. I was explaining, during dinner, how I kept control by out-foxing the ring leaders in my classes. One technique was to allow students to sit wherever they wanted in my classroom for the first few days of the course. I would observe their behaviour during that time, and was able to identify which kids were friends, which ones were chatty, which ones were quiet, and so on. With that established, I would make up a seating plan that separated friends, and surrounded chatty students with those who were not inclined that way. I winked at my dad saying that the more kids were unhappy with the seating plan, the better it proved to be.

My dad looked at me and asked if I had time in my busy day to actually teach these kids anything worthwhile.

That certainly took the wind out of my sails. I felt anger at his words, but I knew he had a point. I knew I was teaching proper skills and understandings in my lessons, but I needed an attitude adjustment when it came to dealing with my kids. In my scheming, I had become a controlling person rather than the warm, helping person I wanted to be in the classroom. Fortunately for me, I passed my evaluation that year and was offered a permanent contract in June of 1975. My principal commented on the improvements he and the superintendent had witnessed, and encouraged me to continue to improve. That felt wonderful, but I was still haunted by his words spoken the previous year, and by my father's criticism. The demon was sustained by those sorts of comments. I didn't know how to manage a class successfully any other way, and it wouldn't be until the following year that I discovered successful teaching depends on much more than strictly enforced rules.

I had yet to drive away my inner fears, and I continued to live with my stomach in knots. I desperately tried to relieve that stress by finding ways to sharpen my skills in the classroom.

At the end of this second year, I found out that half of my schedule the following year would be teaching grade seven and eight History. I was thrilled, but my jubilation was short lived when I ran into my Math department head. She was furious because I would no longer be teaching Math to the grade sevens. I was incredulous — I asked why she wasn't happy that the school's worst Math teacher was hanging up his protractor.

"Because you're one of the best I have in the open area," she sputtered.

"No way," I replied.

"Of all the kids I teach in grade eight, your students are among the few who understand their grade seven work! Don't argue with me!"

She went on to explain that I was very effective teaching Math because I had a lot of trouble mastering the material, and that allowed me to instinctively anticipate where the kids would have trouble. She theorized that I knew exactly what to emphasize and drill. Her words were a direct assault on the demon. Maybe I had done more than just duck the bullet of unemployment.

Third year began happily as I was teaching Canadian History to half of my classes. I had picked up several brand new courses; in fact, of my seven courses, six were new to me. My workload was enormous, and I worked my students very hard too. I was still a pretty stern taskmaster, but my focus was changing. I was no longer worried about discipline in the classroom, because the classroom management techniques applied during the previous year continued to work well. However I was not happy with the quality of the student work I was evaluating, and I wanted that to improve. I didn't realize it then, but this determination placed me on the threshold of what would become my specialty as a teacher: teaching writing skills. At that time there were very few materials available to teach these skills in the content areas of the school curriculum. Students were being taught language skills in their English classes, but they were clearly not demonstrating them in their other courses. Very gradually over the next two years, through trial and error, I began to develop sets of directions on how to write good paragraphs, and later, formal essays. But I'm getting ahead of myself here, because it would still be fifteen more years before these evolved into more formal writing guides. Despite the progress I was making in developing my craft, there was still something important missing.

In November of that year, 1975, our first child was born. Dianna's arrival was characterized by great celebration and it marked the beginning of our new family. I had become a parent. A simple fact, it's true, but the impact was quite profound. Nothing was the same anymore. No longer was I just a husband and a teacher, I was this little girl's father. My dear wife was now a mother as well as a career woman. The new responsibility didn't frighten me, but it did have an impact on my self-image. What I didn't realize was that my little princess, and her two young brothers who followed two and five years later, would change my outlook significantly as a classroom teacher.

As Anne and I nurtured our kids with the help of her family, who lived nearby, I discovered I was slowly

John Fioravanti

becoming a more protective person — as any parent would. Very gradually these paternalistic feelings were making themselves evident in my classroom. I began to see my students in a very different light. They weren't my kids, but their parents entrusted them to our care in the school. I had always been aware of this important responsibility in the classroom, but now I found myself *feeling* it in a way I had never dreamed possible. My feelings for my students had changed. Their success and their well-being became important to me personally. It had become less about me and my struggles, and more about them and theirs. As this new awareness crashed upon my conscious mind, I found myself relating to my students in a different way. The classroom management remained strict, but the classroom became a happier place. I smiled much more in class, and I even laughed at some of the antics of the class clowns. And then, before I knew it, I had become the main class clown!

I remember discussing in class one day my own

experiences as a teen at dances we had in the 1960s. As I warmed to my topic, I suddenly jumped up on top of my desk and demonstrated the bugaloo to a very startled group of students. After we all enjoyed a good laugh, I continued with the lesson. Because the clowning was done in moderation, it worked. The class remained an orderly environment, but my overt humanity softened it into a more comfortable place. My personal experience of parenthood had become another defining development. Outsmarting and controlling students was no longer the priority. The desire I had when I first entered the profession to help students was re-emerging, and this realization gradually became apparent over the next few years.

In retrospect, it is clear that I had inadvertently found the elusive key to dealing with kids in a more caring way. Now I could relate to my students as a real person who was willing to share himself and his personal life. I remember being surprised the first time some students sought me out to talk about personal things that were troubling them. I found myself in new territory, and I had no training when it came to answering those sorts of questions. I needed to learn how to listen effectively. I can only hope that my early, clumsy advice did more good than harm for those kids. It would take me several more years to learn that the most valuable thing I could offer students who confided in me was a willingness to listen and caring support.

By my fourth year, I was involved in advising the student council at the school. That activity also meant helping the council kids plan and stage ten major dances per year. In those days there were no student registration fees paid to support school teams and clubs, so all money had to be raised by the student council, and in a large school like ours, dances were quite lucrative. They were also exhausting. Ten times each year, I would roll into bed no earlier than 3:00 a.m. on a Saturday morning after cleaning up the school and driving home the council kids in two, sometimes three trips, as my car could safely transport just five people at a time.

But I loved it. My clowning in the classroom spilled out at the dances as well. I began appearing as a special guest on stage as Elvis Fioravanti, singing along to Elvis hits the DJ was playing behind me. The kids would gather around the stage screaming like they did at rock concerts. It was all I could do to keep a straight face until the act was finished. I was getting to know these kids much better, and the rapport with my classes was steadily improving too. The rigidity that had characterized my early teaching had softened even more. I even allowed the kids to sidetrack my lessons from time to time when I felt that there was a valuable point to pursue — especially if the detour involved a life lesson. My emotional need to be more than just an academic instructor to my students was being satisfied.

By my sixth year, I was the head student council advisor and I had been appointed the new Social

Sciences head. The department headship meant the world to me since the principal who made the decision was the same one who told me I was his weakest link on staff just five years before. Despite my professional growth and success, the familiar feeling of fear re-emerged now that I had a larger and new slate of responsibilities. I plunged into my department work with a vengeance in a desperate effort to keep my fear of failure at bay.

While grappling with my new responsibilities, I found myself surrounded by shocked and very sad council students who had suddenly lost a staff member who'd been close to them. They were looking to me for answers, and I had none. I listened to their distress and tried to comfort them, but I felt helpless. Only later did I realize two things: first, these kids had turned to me, so I had to believe I had been doing something right when I'd been working with them; and second, just being there for them was a great blessing.

Two years later, that group of council students

had graduated from our school and were attending local public high schools in their grade eleven year. One weekend, a boy who had graduated in the same class was tragically killed in a traffic accident. I didn't know him well, but he was a friend of the council members with whom I had worked closely. On the Monday morning I was teaching in class when the vice-principal came to my door. He said I needed to come to his office right away and that he would cover my class. As I walked past him into the hall, he said that I was to take whatever time was needed. I didn't have a clue what he was talking about. Was I getting the axe? When I opened the door to his office I saw before me a large group of grieving former students who literally threw themselves on me while releasing rivers of tears. They were my council kids. They were devastated beyond words. And they had come to me.

I had no words either. I felt so overwhelmed that all I could do was be there and share their grief. After a long while, they decided they should go home.

I returned to class a changed man.

My rookie years taught me a great number of things. I had made enough blunders to know that excellence in the classroom doesn't happen just because you desire it. Despite my good intentions, hard work, and innate talents, I would never become the teacher I wanted to be without the generous mentoring I received from many staff members at St. Benedict. It became clear that I had to be vigilant in keeping myself open to receiving their suggestions and their good example. But the most significant lesson learned in these years came from my students. In their bewilderment and pain, they turned to me. They were not looking for pearls of wisdom that would fix their world; they turned to me for human comfort because they trusted me to be there for them, to offer understanding and support. I didn't fully realize it then, but that was a glimpse into the heart of teaching.

CHAPTER 5
Women – Can't Live Without Them!

I worked hard to adapt to the leadership role in the Social Science department, but found myself increasingly dissatisfied with the quality of my students' assignments. I knew they were being taught writing skills in their English classes, but those skills were not being demonstrated in my History class. The solution was as simple as it was daunting: I decided to teach the skills I expected the students to demonstrate in their work. My motive stemmed from an unhappy experience I had in my first year at university. The first formal history essay I wrote came back to me with a

C- grade, a far cry from the grades I had earned in my senior high school years. After a discussion with my professor I became aware that I lacked the skills to write a well-organized paper. He directed me to the publication, *Form and Substance* by W.K. Thomas, which I purchased at the university bookstore. Using that book as a model, I taught myself the necessary skills, and for the balance of my university studies, my essays consistently scored grades of A- or better. When I decided to teach, I promised myself I'd do my best to prevent this from happening to my high school History students. While St. Benedict was a junior high, the grade 10 students were our seniors. I taught them the basic skills of formal essay writing, so they could polish those skills when they moved on to other schools to complete the senior grades.

How does a History teacher insert skills into the curriculum? At first, I interrupted the content of my classes with writing skill lessons, and assignments dreamed up to fit them. The results were decidedly mixed: the writing improved, but the assignments did not fit into the flow of the course. Also, there was no clear progression of skill development. I knew I was heading in the right direction, but I felt like I was floundering. When I discussed the problem with colleagues in my school, I was greeted with polite but clearly baffled looks.

Then one evening, while enjoying a social engagement, I got into a discussion with a close friend and very gifted elementary school teacher, Ann O'Donnell-Beckwith. As I described the problem with my attempts to teach writing skills, Ann began to smile and then patted my hand. She told me she knew exactly what was needed and would be delighted to help me. I was hesitant to accept her guidance — thinking that an approach used with grade two classes would not be appropriate for grade ten students — but she was very patient and very wise. She suggested we plan one unit of work together so I could see what it would look like. I decided to humour her, and agreed. This would be one of the most significant turning points in my career, and I had gone forward with it just so I wouldn't hurt a friend's feelings.

I had a lot to learn, but fortunately I had found a great mentor.

As we began the planning session one Saturday morning in January of 1979, Ann explained to me that my approach had to change drastically. Instead of thinking in terms of content to be included in lessons, we needed to first determine the final skill goal for the unit. I agreed, even though I didn't fully understand at first. Together we agreed on the final goal or expectation, and then we broke it down into smaller skill sets to be taught separately. Next, we looked at the important historical concepts that should be covered in the unit. She started smiling. I got nervous again, wondering what was so entertaining. She asked if I could see the next step yet. I felt pretty incompetent — I was lost. She then showed me how we might fit the historical concepts to the skill lessons. As she did, a light finally snapped on in my head.

"Do you mean that we use the History content as a vehicle for the skills?" I asked incredulously.

"Of course!" she exclaimed.

Of course, I thought to myself. I had been putting the proverbial cart before the horse. No wonder my earlier attempts had not worked well. Now I got very excited. Ann started smiling again as my mind raced.

"Then it must follow that the units of a course must be planned towards the achievement of an overall course goal or expectation," I suggested.

"Right again!" she exclaimed gleefully.

All I had to do was use the History in my curriculum as the subject matter for the examples I used when teaching the writing skills… Man, did I feel stupid at not having realized this before. But I also had hope. I told Ann this approach would mean planning my courses from scratch, then figuring out an appropriate final goal for each course, and finally breaking each one down into component skill parts that would be taught within the course units. Good grief!

At that point I knew my final goal for my grade ten students was for them to be able to produce a formal argumentative research essay. Working backwards from there meant lessons in formal language, the expository paragraph, the argumentative paragraph, the five-paragraph argumentative essay, research techniques and sources, and finally, the structure of the larger formal essay along with the necessary skills of documenting sources. The reorganization of the course would involve the insertion of these many skills within the course units and using the appropriate content to carry the skills.

With a great deal of excitement, I decided to share this insight with some colleagues at my school. They smiled at me indulgently, but were really not interested. I was alone, with a lot to figure out. Course outlines provided by the government were not helpful beyond identifying units of study and the content to be taught within each unit. Very little was said about skills to be taught, and there was nothing at all about how to teach these skills. As I searched in vain for guidance, I began to realize I really had no one to turn to. But Ann had given me the principles and the methodology — I had been given a great boost. Now I had to figure out how to break down the skills into logical, teachable steps. With a new challenge and no net, the demon fear of failure stirred its ugly head once again.

For several years I kept the demon at bay by focusing completely on the tasks at hand, instead of the possibility of failure. Some things I tried were successful, while others were not. As I evaluated my students' work, I looked for trends, for common errors that would steer me towards better, more comprehensive skill lessons. I was constantly overhauling my lessons and the student handouts I had prepared. The skill sheet handouts gradually grew in detail and this process continued unabated until November of 2002. As I reflected on some new revisions one day, the realization struck me that my students were teaching me how to teach. I chuckled to myself as I realized that I had become the student. In struggling to outdistance my demon and to achieve excellence in my classroom, I had unwittingly opened myself to the influence of some very effective teachers — my own students! The proof was in their work — it got better each year. I had no idea at that point, but I had only just scratched the surface of the wonders my students could teach me.

Over the next few years during the mid-1980s, I developed a twenty-page guide to writing the formal essay for my grade ten History students. This period also marked the beginning of full government funding for Catholic schools right through grade thirteen or the Ontario Academic Credit — OAC year. Until 1985, the only Catholic high school grades funded were grades 9 and 10, and they received the same dollars as the elementary grades. Grades 11 through 13 in Catholic schools received no funding at all.

After 1985, all Catholic high schools received full secondary school funding for grades 9 through 13. As we transformed the school from junior high school to a full high school curriculum, the importance of training the students in research and formal writing skills became more urgent. My responsibility — the History department — was ahead of the game in that respect, because my close friend and History colleague, Hans vanZandvoort, was eagerly using my writing guides with his students. We were determined, as were the other departments, to make sure that as our grads went on to university, they would be well equipped. Together we collaborated on all aspects of the curriculum, and we worked together like a well-oiled machine. Hans provided the creative genius while I refined his ideas into lessons we piloted, reviewed, and revised. It was a happy partnership and a fruitful one that proved to be very beneficial to our students.

As we were developing all of these senior History courses, I was beset again by fear. This was new ground for the entire staff, so there was no one to act as mentor. I felt even more stressed because I was a department head and therefore the leader. My omnipresent demon was raising his ugly snout once again, causing me to endure constant knots in my stomach and mild anxiety attacks. I could feel my self-confidence slowly evaporating. In my heart I believed that I was delivering a good, skill-based curriculum, but the fear was whispering other things in my mind. I could let all these kids down. If I failed, they wouldn't be ready when they reached university — I would have betrayed them, failed them. It felt like a lot of responsibility.

Doggedly I stayed the course, determined to outrun the fear that I knew was irrational.

In the late 1980s I experienced another major turning point in my career — and quite frankly, in my life. Once again, it was a strong and wonderful woman, who saved me from myself.

Ruth Soltis was an educational assistant on staff,

and had been for a long time. She was older than me with grown children of her own; and she was much beloved by the students. I had organized a History trip to Québec City and asked Ruth to accompany us as a chaperone. It was a long, ten-hour bus ride, but it was one I've never forgotten. She was an easy person to talk to, and students often took advantage of that virtue. I was pleased that we were seated together on that bus ride.

A few hours into the trip, Ruth looked up from the book she was reading, turned towards me and said quietly, "John, what's troubling you? You're very quiet — not yourself."

"Oh, I'm ok, Ruth," I sighed wearily, returning to my own book.

She snorted, and said, "No you're not. But if you'd rather not talk about it, I won't pry."

I smiled sheepishly at her as I closed my book, and said that I don't hide my feelings very well. After some gentle encouragement I opened up, telling her about my insecurities in the classroom as I worked to get our students ready for university. She was stunned. For the first time since I'd known her, Ruth seemed to be at a loss for words. But not for long — her mouth thinned into a grim line and I knew I was in trouble. She glanced around us quickly to make sure there was no one listening, and then she grabbed my arm and ordered me to listen carefully to what she had to say.

"You, my good friend, are the best teacher in this school!" she erupted at me. "How dare you believe otherwise!"

Embarrassed, I laughed and assured her that I truly wished that what she said was true. That earned me another quiet explosion.

"You think because I'm not a teacher, that I don't know what I'm talking about? Over the years I have had occasion to witness every teacher in this school when I sit in on classes and help the students who need support. You know that!" I tried to interrupt, but shushing my response, she continued, "Every educational assistant in this school literally fights to get assigned to students in your classes! And why is that? It's because we love your classes! We see how the kids respond to you and they learn!"

"No kidding?" I responded lamely. Now it was my turn to be stunned. I sat there shaking my head, totally speechless. I respected Ruth an awful lot, and I had no idea that she and her colleagues thought that highly of my work. She paused for a minute letting me digest her words. Then the frown left her face and she smiled warmly.

"I got angry with you because I could see you were so caught up with your anxiety that you needed a good shaking up. Every time I enter your classroom, John, I regret that you never taught any of my own kids."

I thanked her for her support and then we returned to our books. My mind was swimming and I could not concentrate on the words I was reading. Could I be that wrong in my own evaluation of my teaching? I closed my eyes and pondered her words.

Very slowly, I felt myself relax for the first time in a very long while. The thought that kept coming back to me again and again was that this lady had wished I'd taught her children. It was truly exhilarating, and at the same time, humbling.

My conversation with Ruth had quieted my demon, and I felt a greater degree of self-confidence than ever before. For the first time in my career I started arriving at school each day without knots in my stomach. Often I thought of Ruth and gave silent thanks. Years later, after Ruth had retired and I had transferred to St. David High School in Waterloo, I thought about her one evening as I sat before my computer revising (always revising) my essay guide. Suddenly it hit me that this marvelous woman likely had no idea the impact she had wrought in my life. I found her phone number and called. She was very surprised to hear from me. I explained my purpose and thanked her for her kindness and support, telling her how it had made a huge difference in my life. For the second time since I'd known her Ruth was speechless. She was also tearfully happy that I had called to tell her. I had been right — she had no idea that her words on the bus that day had impacted me so profoundly. As we said our goodbyes, I knew I had just given her a nice gift too.

Another lesson learned. Affirmation is a very powerful thing.

Within weeks of that phone call I received three gifts of affirmation totally out of the blue. One young lady I had taught in grade eleven and OAC returned from university to visit and told me her History professor had given her quite a shock when he had returned research papers to her class the week before. With great drama he had decried the horrible drivel he had had to wade through as he tossed their papers back to them. When he came to the last paper, he waved it in the air with a great flourish and proclaimed he had, however, been blessed with a real gem that made the entire ordeal worthwhile.

"This young lady," he stated emphatically, "is the only student among you who has mastered the art of essay writing!" With that he reverently placed my former student's essay on the desk in front of her.

She told me she had been totally overcome. I felt as overcome as she did.

Within days, two more former students visited with similar stories. The last was a young man who had a complaint to lodge with me. I'll call him Brian.

"What's the problem, Brian?" I asked, noting the tense expression on his face.

"It's all your fault, sir. I can't get anything done in my dorm room anymore. Thanks a lot!"

He went on to tell me about being singled out in class by his History professor when essays were returned. Apparently his professor told the other students to ask him to help them learn how to write an essay. Now poor Brian had a constant stream of people knocking on his door asking for assistance. I smiled in response and asked if any of these bothersome souls were attractive young ladies. He grinned a bit at that. I then informed him with a smile that he owed me *big time*. Despite the levity, I was quite moved by his story and concluded I must be doing something right.

Unfortunately, I was at this point still incapable of giving myself credit for my gifts, talents, and accomplishments — at least not without reservations. My fear could be controlled, it seemed, but it couldn't be completely eliminated. Even today, those who are closest to me literally bristle with impatience when I vocalize my doubts in myself. In a way, this problem of self-image has continued to cloud my perception of whom and what I am, and who I am becoming. Luckily though, I have been blessed with people like Ann O'Donnell-Beckwith and Ruth who cared enough and took the time to give me a good shake or a gentle nudge — whichever was required. My students played no small role in this process as well with their precious gifts of affirmation.

♦♦♦

Just a brief aside. In addition to the valuable insights into the outcomes-based planning strategy that would not become trendy until the mid-1990s in Ontario, Ann gave me another invaluable gift over the years. I had been raised in a very chauvinistic society and had never given the women's movement much serious thought. At this time Ann was developing a strong attachment to the goals of feminism and was not afraid to speak her mind. She and her husband Glenn were entertaining my wife, Anne and me at their house. Ann was quite alarmed at how exhausted my Anne appeared and was quick to bring my attention to what should have been obvious to me. After some discussion it became apparent that Anne was getting very little help with the household duties from me and our children. My friend could have hit me over the head with an outraged tirade, but instead, she patiently explained the unfairness involved when a woman had a full-time career outside the home and was doing the majority of the housework as well. I felt pretty awful and vowed that I would carry my fair share and teach our kids to do the same. It is a vow I kept. As the years passed and our friendship with Ann and Glenn blossomed, so did my understanding and appreciation for the importance of gender equity in my home, my classroom, and in society at large. Largely because of the patient tutelage I received from my friend Ann, I share with my students my belief that humanity can never achieve its potential until both genders work together as equal partners in every field of endeavour. The genders are different, but both need the other. Notions of superiority are not only laughable, but are patently self-defeating.

I am living proof of this belief — there are many women who have had major impacts on my life both personal and professional, and they have helped me evolve into the person I am today. But here's the *really* good news: those blessings continue today, and will do so in the future.

CHAPTER 6
Hormones and Respect

In the fall of 1990 I was transferred to my present school, St. David Catholic Secondary School in Waterloo and faced a very new challenge: I was teaching at the same school where my daughter was enrolled as a grade ten student. As the new head of History there, I was teaching several of the senior courses, all of which were single course sections. Sure enough, in the following year, Dianna chose to take the grade eleven course I was teaching. I was pleased because it was one of the reasons why I had asked for the transfer to St. David. I wanted to teach my kids the skills I knew they would need in high school and beyond… but I was also mindful of the fact that most teachers try to avoid teaching their own children. I was excited and concerned at the same time. I knew that I would have to handle this situation very carefully — mainly for Dianna's sake.

My anxiety about that issue was not diminished as Dianna flew into my classroom, waving her timetable at me, gleefully announcing that she was in my class. Well, at least she was not concerned about it. Thankfully, my daughter was a model student who did not require any discipline. On the contrary, my concern had always been that her perfectionism caused her unhealthy stress. We had a great relationship at home and, thankfully, that carried over into the classroom. The only time I became uncomfortable was when she would tell my wife what daddy said in class each day.

The course Dianna took from me that year was 'Society, Challenge and Change', which was an introduction to the fields of Psychology, Sociology, and Anthropology. Throughout the course there were many opportunities for me to illustrate important concepts with real stories from my own family. I realized quickly, though, that I could not share those stories with Dianna's peers in the classroom with us. I also had to consider the fact that Dan was already at St. David in grade nine and Dominic would be following soon, so stories about them wouldn't be a good idea. I had to get very creative in a hurry. So I used stories from my own family growing up in Dundas.

The other major issue that arose was to make sure I evaluated Dianna's work fairly. I didn't want to appear to favor her in any way, and unfortunately, I over-compensated and inadvertently marked her first assignment much harder than I did those of her peers. After that first assignment was returned, I was approached at the end of class by a girl who sat across from Dianna. She asked if she could see me for a few moments at lunch. I agreed, not suspecting what was to follow. When she arrived, she asked me to hear her out and not get angry with her. I had taught this student before in grade nine and we had enjoyed a good relationship, so I smiled and told her that I'd behave myself. She took a deep breath, and then told me she had seen Dianna's paper and that she believed it was far superior to her own; but I had given Dianna a lower grade. She said she thought I had unconsciously marked my daughter's paper by a stricter standard. That deflated my sails in a hurry. I looked this young lady in the eye and told her how much I appreciated her courage and her honesty, then sent her on her way, promising to fix the problem. That night I decided to collect all the papers back the next day, and to remark every paper. I told the class I thought I had made errors in judgment on some of their papers and wanted to re-evaluate them all. I did find errors I had made on other papers besides Dianna's, so I adjusted a number of the marks. I apologized to Dianna at home, telling her I would do my best to be more vigilant in the future. She forgave me and told me she trusted me. I got past that mistake, but I never forgot it.

+ + +

We both survived Dianna's grade eleven year quite gracefully, but I was still struggling to fit in at my new school. The year before, my first year at St. David, none of the students there knew me and I had felt like a rookie all over again. The lack of familiar ground let the old anxiety return to haunt me, though soon I'd begin to gain that confidence back, thanks to my essay teaching method. I always explained to my students that my structural formula for an essay was not the only method that can be used, but I insisted they follow my directions until they had mastered the basics of organization. From my own personal experience in university, and that of former students, I knew my formula worked well. I remember during that first year teaching one young lady (I'll call her Joan) who liked history and was in both of my OAC History courses. She was very bright, quite self-assured and assertive. She was forever challenging my essay writing expectations, because she found them very restrictive.

I would smile at her and say she needed to prove to me she could master my method of essay writing, later she could write any way she wanted at university. She was not happy with me. A year later she returned to pick up her younger brother who was writing a final exam in the cafeteria where I was presiding. As the students were exiting the room, Joan walked over to me and gave me a big hug. She told me that I had saved her life. I was very surprised and embarrassed.

She laughed at the expression on my face and explained she was enrolled in a very demanding concurrent program at Queen's University in Kingston, Ontario, and that her essays had pulled her through the first semester. After she left, I scratched my head, totally befuddled. I was sure that this girl really didn't like me at all the year before.

The surprise I had experienced at the hands of Joan was surpassed when another former student came to visit. I'll call him James. This young man had transferred from a private high school for his OAC year. He was a tall, handsome young man who was very bright as well, and a hard worker to boot. As did Joan, James took issue with my essay methods. In a respectful manner, he fought me tooth and nail every step of the way throughout the course. He complied with my wishes, but he made it clear that he was just humouring me. James wrote some terrific papers and graduated with top marks. One day, several years later, I was eating my lunch in my classroom when the secretary called over the P.A. system asking me to meet a visitor in the main office. When I entered the office, there was James with a great big smile and hand outstretched to shake mine. We then went out to the hallway and he explained why he was visiting.

"I was thinking about you this morning," he began. "You see, I finished my degree and I was thinking about how much I owed you for my success at university, and it suddenly occurred to me that you didn't have any idea! So I came here today to thank you and to ask you something."

I felt stunned, but I asked him to go on.

"Please sir," he began, "don't ever stop doing what you did for me!"

That said, he bade me goodbye and left the building. As I made my way back to my classroom, I began to smile and I thought of Ruth.

That's a promise I can keep, I thought, and I found I had a bit of a spring to my step.

The sense of elation I felt as a result of James' visit was to be short-lived. I was teaching my daughter's OAC History class one day, and the topic was President Teddy Roosevelt's foreign policy tactics as they related to Canada at the turn of the twentieth century. After explaining his "gunboat diplomacy", I went on to inform the class that his tactics were also known as "Big Stick Diplomacy", only it came out of my mouth as "Big Dick Diplomacy"! My daughter screamed out "DADDY!" The entire class exploded in laughter while I stood there totally humiliated. As the hilarity continued I began to laugh too. How would

I ever live this one down? Would the school board ever let me teach again? When Anne heard about my performance at the dinner table that evening, she was worried sick that I would be hauled before the principal and disciplined. Thankfully, that didn't happen.

As I thought about this performance later, I realized that there was another valuable lesson here. I had to stop taking myself so seriously. My Freudian slip, although embarrassing, had somehow made me more human in the eyes of my students. More importantly, I began to see that I had adopted a more prim and proper demeanor at St. David, probably because of my anxiety at being the new teacher at school. I needed to return to the more relaxed style I had developed at St. Benedict. Not only was I learning new lessons from my students, but I was also relearning old lessons as well.

Fitting in at St. David was tough in the early years, despite the fact that this staff was quite warm and welcoming. The challenge of being at a new school was coupled with another that almost brought me to my knees. Earlier in my career I had experienced a positive turning point when I became a father. Now I found that being a parent of three teenagers was causing me psychological stresses I never dreamed possible. What was wrong with my kids? Absolutely nothing. They were good kids. But they were teenagers. And the students in my classroom were teenagers. I had been teaching teens for many years; now I was living with three of my own, so I was dealing with teenaged hormones twenty-four hours a day, seven days a week.

Home had once been my refuge, the place where I could escape each evening and each weekend to the different world of my young family. That respite allowed me to recharge my emotional batteries. I would be able to return to my classes each day with renewed patience and understanding. Now there was no respite. There was no recharging of the emotional batteries. Psychologically, I was feeling burnt out.

I remember losing my cool one day with an OAC class. One thing that really pushes my buttons is the arrival of students to class after the lesson has begun. On this day, three students arrived late and interrupted the class at three separate intervals. Normally I'm annoyed at the interruption because it derails my thought process and thus, the flow of the lesson. On this occasion the three offenders seemed oblivious to the fact that they had done anything wrong. Their attitude seemed to scream out that rules were for everyone else, but not for them. I lost it. I screamed at those poor kids for at least five minutes. For my grand finale, I threw my text on my desk with a bang, and told them to work on note making for the balance of the class. You could have heard a pin drop, and the silence lasted until the final bell. The students slunk wordlessly out of class.

The next day, this same group crept quietly into the classroom, on time, and sat in silence while they waited for me to begin. I smiled at them and asked why everyone was so solemn. A big football player at the back asked if I was ok. I assured him that I was. I asked him the same question in return. He hesitated, and then said that he hoped that I was ok after yesterday, saying that my anger had really scared all of them. Well, that revelation completely shocked me. As I made eye contact with everyone in the room, I realized he spoke for every last one of them. I felt totally ashamed of myself. I took a deep breath, and I apologized for my behaviour and I told them that I had no excuse. I also promised them that they would never be subjected to that in my classroom again.

It was a painfully embarrassing moment for me; yet it gave me pause to perform some much needed personal introspection. As I berated myself for this outburst of temper, I also realized these kids had given me an opportunity to pause and to learn. It wasn't the first time I had shouted at a class, but I had never realized before just how frightening it was for the students. I was scarier than I had ever dreamed possible. Was I scarring these kids? As I pondered the situation and the inner turmoil that had brought it to a head, it became clear that there was a larger, more significant issue here. The root of my problem was far more fundamental than a loss of temper in the classroom. It really had more to do with how I saw my students, and equally important, what I expected of them. In time I came to see that those expectations were impossible because I was not looking at these young people as unique individuals. Oh yes, I had always accepted their uniqueness as an intellectual concept, but I had not internalized it in my heart. For too many years I viewed students in the class as a collective blob of teenaged hormones, but now that my own kids were teens, I began to recognize the different paths each of my students tried to take.

My reactions to infractions like lateness had been exacerbated by my incomplete understanding of self as a person and as educator — my inability to see my students for themselves. The proof of this was evident in my expectation that if I provided good teaching, modeled good work habits, and encouraged them to strive for excellence, students would simply respond and succeed. I was not accepting them as they were, I was expecting them to become what I wanted them to become. I was not sensitive enough to determine how each student was developing as a person, and then proceed to meet their needs. In other words, I viewed them as young learning machines instead of flesh and blood persons in their own right, with their own personal circumstances, histories, and demons. How could these students possibly trust me to guide them if I could not respect and love them as they were?

Later I would discover that the key is respect for my students. Love is important, of course, but the acceptance of one's unique personhood guides the love and gives it impact. These realizations came to me very gradually, and very painfully. I felt pain because I could see where my own shortcomings had somewhat short-changed the kids entrusted to me. Although I worked hard at my craft, I was forever focusing on my faults — and that drove me to eliminate the deficiencies within myself. How do I accept these kids as they are when I know so little about them? The answer to this question was to elude me for a few years yet. Not being able to immediately grasp the answer increased my frustration, but I know now that the fog was gradually being lifted from my eyes. Unknowingly I was getting closer to understanding the heart of teaching.

CHAPTER 7
An Angel on my Lapel

In June of 1995 I was celebrating the end of my twenty-second year in the classroom, and the end of my fourth year at St. David in Waterloo. Although I was quite happy in this school, I finished the school year with a strong feeling of foreboding. Ontario had just elected a new Progressive Conservative government led by Premier Mike Harris, who had promised to overhaul the education system and to obliterate the debt accrued by earlier Liberal and NDP governments. My concern stemmed from the fact that educational reform would be very expensive, and the government would be cutting spending in order to reduce the provincial debt. I figured there would be sharp cuts in educational spending as a result, but I was afraid of wage rollbacks as well.

The Tories had a relatively simple plan to carry out their educational reform: first discredit the teachers of Ontario, then push through their reform package believing the voters would pay little heed to the warnings made by 'selfish, under-worked, overpaid' teachers who were led by 'union thugs'. The strategy continued for two years as war was waged in the media between teacher associations (union thugs) and the Ontario government. Newspaper coverage seemed to favour the government, and the letters to the editor in the local newspaper supporting the government outweighed those supporting the teachers. Our profession was most definitely under siege, and it was taking its toll on us emotionally as we struggled to carry on in the classroom. Our staff room was a tense and gloomy place. I knew there was little we could do about public opinion, and that both saddened and angered me.

By 1997 the government began to put forward its reform package, which led to a two-week protest by Ontario teachers who left their classrooms. When the protest failed to derail the Tory plans for reform, it was clear the war was lost. The inner turmoil I was experiencing throughout this period coloured everything I did. The atmosphere in our staff room was doing more to intensify my feelings of helplessness than to dispel them. I was becoming very negative and it was distracting me from my purpose as a teacher. At that point I was emotionally as far away from the heart of teaching as I could be. I knew I could do nothing about educational reform, nor could I repair the negative public perception of the teaching profession. As I considered the hopelessness of the situation, I became aware that my turmoil was having an impact on my classroom. My lessons had lost their zip — I was going through the motions, but I was not emotionally present for my students. I was all tangled up with a political battle and lost in a jungle of negativity. This was not good.

This awareness actually compounded my inner turmoil as guilt entered the mix. I found myself participating in the negative discussions around the lunch tables in the staff room; and then I'd go back to class in a very combative mood. I wasn't shocked out of this vicious cycle until I confronted a student who told the class that the Tories were quite justified in putting teachers in their place. Fortunately, I didn't lose control, but I did strenuously put forward my point of view. Afterward, I sat at my desk with my head in my hands wondering whatever happened to the History lesson I had been prepared to teach that day. It got lost. No, I got lost, and I had been lost for quite some time.

Whatever happened to the guy who was searching for excellence in the classroom? What about being there for the students? I knew I had to get back on track.

My solution bewildered my colleagues even as it led me ever closer to discovering the heart of teaching. I wish I could say I planned it that way, but I didn't. As I analyzed the problem I was facing, it became clear that the more time I spent in the staff room discussing the ongoing war with the Harris government, the more negative I was becoming. My colleagues at the time were wonderful educators — really caring individuals — and I didn't blame them for my negativity. I blamed myself, and my inability to leave that stuff behind when I went back to class. So my solution was simple: avoid the staff room and the inevitable discussions. I knew that would not magically turn things around, but I hoped it would be a step in the right direction.

I began to take my morning coffee to my classroom. I ate my lunch in my classroom. I spent my preparation period in my classroom. I went to the staff room only to use the photocopier. It was lonely, but I was getting lots more work done at school, and I left my door open so students could come in and use the four computers I had at the back of the room, though that seldom happened. Very gradually, I noticed I was thinking less and less about the political problems that had overwhelmed me, and my focus on my students and on my lessons was returning.

After spending the better part of the first semester that year in self-imposed isolation, I quickly found that the new semester, just beginning, was to be very different. A few days into the new term, I was eating my lunch in my classroom when several grade nine girls who I had taught in the previous semester walked into the room to visit. They wanted to know why I was eating alone there, so I told them it gave me an opportunity to get some marking done. I asked how they liked their new classes. Without hesitation, they stated that they were ok, but they really missed my History class. I thanked them for their kindness. One asked if I minded if they visited me from time to time. I told them they were welcome to visit any time they liked. A second girl wanted to know if they could bring their lunch and eat in my classroom with me, since I had never allowed any food or drink into the room. I told them they were welcome to do so as long as there was no mess. As they left, I smiled and thought that even if they never returned, it was nice to be missed.

The very next day those same girls showed up at my door with not only their lunches, but a few other students as well. That day we ate as a group and swapped stories. This continued into the following week, and more students were joining our unofficial lunch club — some of them were not even former students of mine. The lunch club continued every single day of the semester. I did not eat alone again that year.

Since I always kept my classroom door open, it was clear to all who passed my door that Room 107 was becoming a happening place. There was a core group who came every day, some others who came periodically, and others still who came and asked to use the computers. On any given day there would be a dozen to twenty students camping in 107 at lunch. I remember one day in particular when a female staff member came to my door and hesitated in the doorway. I waved her in and greeted her warmly. She asked me quietly why I no longer came to the staff room at lunchtime. She was concerned that I was angry or upset with my colleagues. Why would I willingly turn my classroom into a student lunchroom every single day? I assured her that I was not shunning the staff, and that I kept the room open for any kids who needed a quiet place to work or to use the computers. I told her that it also allowed me to be more available to students for extra help. Obviously still puzzled, she looked at me, smiled sweetly and left. I realized then that in my attempt to solve one problem, I had likely created another one. Although I did not want to distance myself from my colleagues, I knew that the lunch club was doing wonders for my emotional well-being. Closing down Room 107 at lunch was not an option.

✦✦✦

Tragedy struck the school that second semester as one of my first semester students was killed in a car accident one weekend near her home. She was not a regular in the lunch club, but the core members had been close friends with her. On the Monday morning before classes started, very distraught and tearful students from the club came to my door and enveloped me in a group hug. For the second time in my career I found myself feeling helpless in the midst of abject misery. All I could do was hug them and be there. This time I felt the grief too, because the student who died, Jennifer, had been a favourite of mine. As I navigated my way through this whirlwind of grief, I felt a sense of peace in that my experience before had taught me that just being present and available to others in grief was really all I could do. Grieving is a process that takes time, and no words — no matter how well intentioned — can fix it or make it go away. That same night I found myself in the hospital with a kidney stone attack. I ended up staying there for two days. My principal visited on the second day to tell me that Jennifer's parents had asked that I be a pall bearer at the funeral the next day.

"Are you serious?" I asked.

"Come on John," he replied, "you were one of her favourite teachers."

I told him to thank the parents for me, but I doubted whether I'd be released in time the following day. He assured me that he'd have it covered if I couldn't get there. After he left, I felt so honoured and so unworthy. I wasn't about to forgive myself for falling into that black pit the previous two years.

When I returned to class I found myself being welcomed by my students and the lunch club kids, who were understandably still pretty subdued. The following week, the school hosted a memorial service for Jennifer and I was able to offer my condolences to her parents in person. Jennifer's mother hugged me and gave me a pin to wear on my lapel. It was an angel pin. She explained that they had given them to the other pall bearers at the funeral as well. I thanked her, and I wore that pin every day at school for the next four years until Jennifer's class graduated.

The political wars that have coloured more than the last half decade of my career had left an indelible mark on my soul. The fear, the anger, and later the frustrated outrage, had put my journey into jeopardy. And yet ironically, the resulting personal crisis had led me to an isolation from which I was rescued by a group of grade nine students who were looking for rescue as well. I had no idea at the time what the lunch club in 107 would mean to my career, or to my life. But I knew it was very precious to me. Unknowingly, those kids had thrown me a lifeline, and the tragic death that followed made me realize my responsibility to them was as important now as ever before. Putting that angel pin on my lapel or my sweater each day reminded me of what was really important. External pressures like political conflict and reform will inevitably intrude upon the classroom, but the lesson I learned here is that I must 'let go' of negative feelings about things I can't control. I have to keep my attention on those things I can control — how I manage a classroom and interact with the most important people there, my students.

CHAPTER 8
The Lunch Club Phenomenon

During the summer of 1997 I did a lot of soul searching. My twenty-fourth year in the classroom had been fraught with emotional ups and downs that seemed more like deep canyons and perilously high mountains. The demon within that had plagued me for several decades was fairly well contained. I no longer worried about being found incompetent, or completely failing my students. During the previous semester my principal had unceremoniously interrupted an interview I was conducting with two parents. He stood beside me, facing the parents, and told them that I was the most dynamic teacher he had on staff. Then he apologized for interrupting and sauntered away. I turned crimson and was at a loss for words.

"Wow!" the father said as he watched my principal leave.

"I paid him to say that," I responded, trying to recover with some levity.

"I don't think so," replied the mother, "my son tells me the same thing. As a matter of fact, we came in tonight just to meet you."

Once again I felt that feeling of unworthiness. And as I reviewed the incident, I had to admit the demon wasn't done with me yet. Intellectually, I knew I was doing a good job in the classroom, and yet I still was slow to give myself credit. Was it false humility? I was to discover over the next few years that it was something else — a chronic habit of viewing myself with a jaded eye.

When the new school year began, I wondered whether the lunch club kids would return to my digs in 107. I didn't have to wait long to find out — they returned immediately. As September wore on, I noticed that membership in the club was changing. Several of the core group had returned, but some were hanging out elsewhere with their friends. I also noticed that new kids were drifting into my room and making themselves at home. Something else had changed: there were kids drifting in occasionally for the sole purpose of getting extra help with assignments. I also had some former students arriving on my doorstep wanting help with written assignments from other subject areas. What I found fascinating about that was that the kids who were there just to eat and hang out would drift away from my desk when someone wanted help — without being asked. It was so subtle I didn't notice it happening at first, but it was such a powerful sign of respect from them that I felt blessed.

For the next two years, the lunch club continued on that way, and while the membership changed, the atmosphere didn't. It was a rewarding place for me to spend my lunch hour, and more was still to come.

In the fall of 1999, I found myself teaching English to grade ten students for the first time in almost twenty years. That was fortuitous, as it caused me to meet a young man who would have a profound impact upon my journey to the heart of teaching. His name is Kenneth Tam and I was to discover that he was the most gifted student ever to sit in my classroom. He was quiet, soft spoken, and somewhat shy — understandable as he was new to the school, having transferred to us from Alberta. I remember threatening another student one day with a weeklong membership in my lunch club. He didn't believe the club existed until a couple of other students piped up and verified that 107 rocked at lunchtime. I laughed and told the class that it was true and anyone was welcome to drop by and check it out. Before long I noticed that Kenneth had taken me up on that offer. He never left during the next three years. He wasn't alone, either, as new people were coming by from the four English classes I taught that year. The lunch club was growing and changing. I didn't realize at the time that it was changing me as well.

At one point our new principal wandered into 107 at lunch, surveyed the room from the doorway, approached me and asked me to see him during my preparation period. I didn't know what he wanted, but I had a feeling he might try to shut down the lunchtime gathering. As it turned out I was wrong about that, but he did want an explanation for turning 107 into a lunchroom. After describing the history of the club and its constant state of evolution, he sat back in his chair and smiled at me.

"You do this every day at lunch?" he inquired in a disbelieving tone.

"Yes, I'm there whether the kids show up or not," I replied matter of factly.

"Why do you do this?" he shot back.

I thought carefully before I replied, "I believe there

are some good things happening in 107 at lunch. There are a lot of different reasons why kids are drawn to the lunch club. Some like the atmosphere and like to hang out there with their friends. Others know that I'll help them with assignments and such. There are students who just come to use the computers when the ones in the Library are full. And there are some who feel ostracized in the general population and have found a comfort zone in 107. And I benefit too."

"How do you benefit from this lunch club when it keeps you away from your colleagues at lunchtime?" he asked in a sympathetic tone.

"The kids keep me focused on my primary role here," I replied, "and they provide a positive atmosphere which gives me peace and strength as well. Whether they know it or not, they give me positive reinforcement just by walking through that door. I can only hope I'm giving something positive back in return."

He considered that for a moment, then nodded and gave me his blessing to continue to keep 107 open at noon. He went a step further and said he would write it up in my file as extra-curricular activity — lunchtime mentoring.

To be perfectly frank, I had not thought of the lunch club as 'mentoring', although the term did fit what was really going on in 107. I realized I had been enjoying the experience so much that I hadn't given the mentoring component much consideration. I had always viewed myself as the major beneficiary of the lunch club. After all, these kids made my daily lunchtime a very enjoyable experience. All I did was respond positively. I didn't structure the activity. I supervised the activities going on, socialized with the kids as they drifted in and out, and helped those who asked for assistance. From my perspective, it was no big deal.

A few years after my conversation with the principal, a young grade ten student named Maria came to me at lunchtime, clearly distraught. Maria was older than the other kids in my grade ten History class because she was an exchange student from Colombia studying here to improve her English. As she sat in the chair beside me at the desk, she covered her face with her hands and cried quietly. The lunch club kids responded quickly and either left the room or moved to the back rows, giving us some privacy. It turned out Maria had to be part of a group presentation in another course and had been told by her group that they wanted her to be absent that day because they feared her speaking skills would damage the presentation. I told her she was an excellent student and that all the teachers understood her presence in the school. I told her how much I admired her courage in class and her determination to learn. After explaining why I believed the evaluation process would not harm the marks of her group members, she relaxed somewhat. We talked about hurtful remarks and personal maturity. My goal was to have her leave the room feeling good about herself, but I wasn't convinced I had helped much.

Maria returned to the lunch club just one more time — her last day at St. David before she returned home. She gave me a piece of paper with the following note:

Mr. Fioravanti:

Gratitude is the memory of the soul. That is why today I would like to say thanks for all the lessons you taught me, for all the knowledge you tried to transmit to me and also for giving me the glorious hand I needed to be more confident about myself.

To Colombia, I am taking the best of the memories of this course and also, a very big bag filled with advice, smiles, lessons, satisfaction, appreciation and kindness.

Thanks for contributing to my life.

Sincerely,
Maria

Understandably, I was stunned by this note of thanks. I was not only surprised, but humbled as well. I became acutely aware that most of time I had no clear idea about the impact I had on my students — both in the classroom and the lunch club.

By this time, there were students who came to 107 in the morning before classes as well as at lunch. Kenneth Tam, introduced earlier, was one of those students along with some of his friends. In his grade eleven and twelve years, he took my World History (Ancient and Medieval) course as well as the OAC Canadian course. Kenneth and I shared a passionate interest in science fiction in general and *Star Trek* in particular. I encouraged my senior students to express their research in creative formats, which turned out to be a perfect fit for Kenneth's talents. He was an excellent writer, a thorough researcher, and his creative offerings literally blew me away. Then I discovered he was using much of his free time in school to work on a series of science fiction novels — a project that had been ongoing throughout his high school years. A couple of things struck me about this. He was a very bright and talented person who treated everyone with great respect and never talked down to his peers. He shared that project with a few friends, but he never drew attention to himself because of it. Throughout Kenneth's years at St. David, I thoroughly enjoyed his presence and that of his close friends. At the same time, I wondered why he spent so much time in 107. Quite frankly, I didn't see that I had much to offer him. Later, that opinion would be challenged quite vehemently.

I didn't know it then, but the lunch club would gradually disappear after Kenneth's class graduated. The original group who started the whole thing was graduating as well. The next two years after that saw the lunch club reduced to two or three students, then two, and finally just one. It was the end of a chapter in my career, and its loss didn't sit well with me. I thought sadly of the silly daily ritual when I would bundle my lunch trash into a plastic bag and then toss it across the room into the garbage pail. If I hit it without touching the rim of the pail I would exclaim amid the applause, "Nothing but bag!" If I missed, there were good natured jeers. One student even kept track of the daily tosses and kept a running percentage. When he graduated, the lunch club was no more — he was the only student who came to 107 at lunch that last semester.

Although I struggled to overcome it, the loneliness weighed heavily on my heart. I knew there was no point in trying to resurrect the club since I had not created it in the first place. I began to wonder if I had erred in some way. Perhaps I had changed. Well, I had changed, but my morose misgivings indicated that I had missed the nature and point of that change. In fact, it would take another few years before I would be able to put the lunch club phenomenon into proper perspective.

My disappointment did not cause me to close 107 at lunch so I could eat in the staff room. There were still occasions when students would drift in to use the computers or get some extra help, and when that didn't happen, I spent the time marking the never-ending stream of papers. I was finding myself being less and less productive when I marked papers during the evening hours, so getting the marking done at school became a higher priority than socializing with staff. This was illustrated also when I adopted the practice of arriving at school earlier in the mornings to use that time for marking. This is not to say that I shunned the staff at my school. We have a great staff of dedicated women and men with whom I interacted quite positively throughout the years. Despite the fact that they don't see me eating in the staff room, they have been very supportive of my activities in 107 and I feel blessed to be working among them.

The following year Kenneth returned for a visit to fill me in on his first year at university. He and his parents had formed a publishing company, Iceberg

Publishing, to publish a book penned by Kenneth's mother, Jacqui Tam, as well as the science fiction series that Kenneth had written. He wanted me to help him arrange the launch of the first *Equations* novel in the Library at St. David, and to serve as MC during the launch. I was delighted with the news and readily agreed. Afterwards I got very nervous about my role as MC and dealing with the television people who would be reporting on the event. The launch went well, and I got the opportunity to meet many of Kenneth's friends and professors. As it turns out, one of his History professors was a former student of mine back at St. Benedict. She laughed and told me that Kenneth often spoke about a high school teacher who taught him how to write a formal essay.

"I should have known right away," she said. "After all, you did the same for me!"

But the most significant part of the evening for me came as I spoke to Kenneth's father, Peter, while Kenneth was signing books. He thanked me for everything I had done for Kenneth during his years at St. David. I said to him that since Kenneth was so brilliant, I probably didn't teach him much. He took my arm, looked me straight in the eye and said quietly, but vehemently, "You may not know what you've done for Kenneth, but believe me sir, you left a significant mark on that young man, and we're very grateful!"

You probably could have pushed me over with a feather. I didn't argue the point, and I thanked him for his kind words. I went home that night feeling very humbled.

As I think about the evolution of the lunch club and its impact upon me, I ponder why students like Maria and Kenneth, and all of the others, would spend so much time with me in 107, or seek me out when they were troubled. Had the lunch club been just an escape for a troubled teacher and for students looking to alleviate some boredom in their lives? No, the unofficial club lasted over six years and its membership was in constant flux. There was more to it than that. Sometimes it had been just a fun place to be — especially when I tossed my garbage, or fired elastics at the picture of my least favourite prime minister at the back of the room. We laughed together at such times, we griped together at other times, and we cried together too. We had serious moments when discussing personal issues, political events, or horrific terrorist attacks. Sometimes nothing more important was happening than a game of hangman on the blackboard behind me.

As I see it now, the lunch club resulted in the building and nurturing of relationships — some of which continue to the present day. At the time I did not fully understand its significance. Now I believe this is actually what Peter Tam was trying to communicate to me on that wonderful evening of Kenneth's book launch. Even though I didn't really understand it that night, the experience was a balm for my troubled soul.

CHAPTER 9
The Book that Tripped me

In an earlier chapter, I talked about my quest to help students develop writing, thinking, and research skills through the History courses I taught. By the time I left St. Benedict in June of 1990, I had developed a detailed formal essay guide sporting over twenty pages of text and examples. I continued to utilize the guide with my senior classes at St. David, and it evolved into a more detailed manual. I had shown the manual to a couple of History professors at the University of Waterloo in the late eighties before I left St. Benedict; their reaction was quite positive, so I was confident in continuing its use. I was also determined to ensure that it was improved with annual revisions.

During the early 1990s I picked up an idea from Rob Holowack, head of our Technology Department, who had developed a series of 'Just-In-Time' skill books that he was using in his courses. Rob had developed software templates to create these booklets and they were being used by technology teachers at our school and at the region's other four Catholic high schools. Rob was very generous with his time and he supported my use of his software templates to develop my own Just-In-Time skill books. The booklets were uploaded to the school computer network where all students and staff could access and print them. I developed skill books for my junior level classes, and I transformed the formal essay guide into a series of smaller Just-In-Time booklets for my senior students. I was surprised one day to discover that Rob and a few other Technology teachers had their students access some of my booklets to help them complete written components of Technology assignments. Before long,

I was informed that a handful of teachers from three other school departments were accessing and using them as well. It felt good to be making a contribution to courses across the curriculum. Of course, this was before 'literacy' became sexy in educational circles.

By the late 1990s I had transformed my series of booklets into another format, and I called them 'FioraSkill Books'. By this time I had seven and was using them in all of my History courses. They evolved annually as the earlier essay guides had. That was one of my summertime tasks.

In the spring of 2002 I met a former principal from the Mississauga area who was mentoring student teachers from one of the faculties of education in Buffalo. Her role was to mentor student teachers during their practicum weeks, so I met her when she arrived in 107 to see a student teacher I was assigned at the time. She spotted one of my FioraSkill books, perused it, and asked if I had others. After she looked at them, she told me about a publisher who would be interested. Apparently, this publisher was looking for skill materials written for students. I followed up, the publisher offered me a contract, and by November of that same year, he published *Getting It Right in History Class* which incorporated my seven skill books as separate chapters plus two new chapters I wrote for the book. Pretty heady stuff! Besides the ego boost — which was substantial — I was happy to have this improved tool to use in my own classroom.

I was floating on the proverbial cloud nine enjoying the ego trip immensely. It was a real kick putting this book into my students' hands each semester and noting their facial expressions as they noticed the name of the author. It shouldn't have made a difference in their level of trust in following my skill development directions, but it did. I also discovered through guidance staff that some parents had asked for their children to be placed in my grade ten History classes because they were pleased with the teaching I gave to their older siblings. This was really making me feel very good about myself

— a very far cry from my early days in the classroom!

What more could I want? Sure, the lunch club was disintegrating at this point, but I had reached a nice level of professional accomplishment. Do you hear another 'but' coming? Despite the stroking my professional ego had experienced, I was not really happy. I struggled to get a handle on the root of my disquiet, but I just could not figure it out. I knew I was disappointed about the disintegration of the lunch club in the aftermath of the publication of my book. I couldn't see how the two might be linked. To this day, I'm not sure that they were. I also acknowledged that I shared my colleagues' dissatisfaction with educational reform foisted on us by the Harris government. I recall one morning I was in the staff room with some colleagues photocopying materials when a few teachers with grade nine classes were complaining about the new evaluation system introduced that year. I would not face that reality until the following year when reform reached grade ten courses, but I was studying the new system, hoping to get a handle on it ahead of time. I commented to the teachers doing the complaining that I thought it was ridiculous and unfathomable as well. That prompted one veteran teacher to look me in the eye and ask what hope the rest of the staff had if I couldn't figure it out.

That gave me pause. Was that the cause of the growing realization that the joy I used to know in the classroom was dissipating quickly? At that point I was upset that the new evaluation system was so difficult to understand. Later, after using it for a few years, I was convinced it was not an improvement over the old system — and that made me angry.

Unable to put my finger on the problem, I drifted through 2003 and 2004, doing what I had been doing for decades, but enjoying it less and less. My thoughts were focusing more and more on retirement as I closed in on that magic 85 factor. When a teacher's age added to her or his years of service add up to 85, then that teacher may retire without penalty to their pension. All I talked about was retiring and looking for a new career to start. I was thinking that perhaps I could find some of that lost joy in another field — abandon education entirely. My wife, Anne, was becoming increasingly alarmed with this talk. She didn't understand what was going on, and neither did I. I couldn't come up with a satisfactory explanation for my plan to 'get out of Dodge' as soon as I became eligible in 2004. In class one morning, I warned the students that I was eligible to retire in another week and that they should be nice to me or I might retire and let the supply teacher who would replace me mark their essays. I was kidding, but they apparently took my words to heart. While I was marking a paper at lunch, one of my female students tiptoed into the room and stood before me. I looked up and greeted her with a smile. Then I noticed that she was wearing a very troubled expression. She asked me if I really planned to leave the following week. It was clear that my kidding around had not been received that way. I then noticed that she was a spokesperson for a larger group waiting just outside my door. I invited them to enter and explained that I would never leave any class in the lurch mid semester — especially not their class. Before they left, I apologized for alarming them. In the privacy of my empty classroom, I put my head down on my desk and berated myself for being so careless with these kids.

Unfortunately, my lack of motivation continued. One day in frustration, Anne exclaimed, "Why would you want to leave the classroom? You are a great teacher, and you know that! You can do so much more good if you stay!"

That gave me pause as I mentally reviewed my career. She wasn't wrong; she rarely is. So what was happening to me? Why was I so intent to hang up my chalk? Was I disappointed that I had failed in my quest? Had I failed? As these questions swirled unendingly around in my head, I decided that quitting the classroom would not help me get to the root of my spiritual malaise. I knew I was disappointed that my own school board had not acknowledged my book nor had they encouraged other schools in our board to adopt it. Was this the real problem? I recoiled from this thought in horror. What would *that* say about me? I was appalled at myself for wallowing around in self-pity and decided to prove to myself that I was better than that. I couldn't retire thinking that I had failed. What I didn't realize then was that I had made a date with destiny.

Once I allowed the date of eligibility for early retirement to pass in December of 2004, I became determined to somehow rediscover the joy I once had in the classroom. Fortunately, that year I had a very wonderful crop of grade ten students in both semesters, and we clicked! As my emotional bond developed with these classes, I found myself relaxing and actually having fun again. I wasn't jumping up on my desk to demonstrate the bugaloo any more — getting too old for that — but there was a wholesome banter happening between the students and myself that had been missing in recent years. Although the lunch club did not reinvent itself, I was being visited now and then at lunchtime by many of these kids. I found myself coming home with a lighter heart most days, and I began to hope that this newfound happiness in the classroom wasn't all smoke and mirrors. As it turned out, 2005-2006, my thirty-third year, was when the elusive answers I'd been seeking for so long made themselves apparent.

CHAPTER 10
The Answers are Within

As the school year began in September of 2005, St. David was undergoing the first phase of a two-year renovation plan. Much of it was happening in my corridor as a new hospitality room was being prepared at one end of the corridor, while a new wing of four classrooms was under construction at the other end. I had been informed that 107 would be renovated into a new specialty classroom during the second phase, and I would be moving down the hall into one of the new rooms. On the one hand, I was excited at the prospect of getting a brand new room with air conditioning; on the other hand, I realized it was the end of an era as I had worked in 107 for over fifteen years.

The first semester was utter chaos. During the first two months the noise drove us crazy as we tried to carry on with our work in 107. Once the winter set in, the temperature in the corridor outside my door plunged as all that separated us from the new construction outside was a flimsy particle board partition. That forced me to keep the door of my room closed to retain adequate heat, but with no fresh air coming into the room, the air quality became unbearable. Knowing the end was in sight, I encouraged my students to soldier on to the end of the semester. It was a hardship we endured together and it created a warm camaraderie that transformed an uncomfortable situation into one where we bonded in a special way.

As this semester was ending I found myself feeling very tired physically. The stresses of the renovations were partly responsible, but I was aging and my personal struggles with diabetes during the past ten years were also contributing factors. So, naturally, thoughts of retirement began to intrude once again. I shrugged these thoughts aside, hoping that I would get my second wind with the new semester. After all, my quest to be the best teacher I could be was not yet finished.

D-Day came in February 2006 when the new classrooms opened and I made the move into my new digs — Room 108B — a temporary designation until the next phase of renovations would be completed. Happily, I got lots of visits from former students who wanted to check out the new room. Even better, my new batch of students were the kind of kids that I bonded with very quickly. I always worry when the semester changes and I get new classes. Throughout my career, I've been able to bond well with most classes, but there have been a few exceptions. At these times I was always quick to blame myself, but now I believe that these instances of limited bonding aren't anyone's fault. Allowing myself to feel guilt about it was both pointless and counter-productive. As it turned out, I didn't need to worry about the new students — they walked through the door and into my heart.

I was still a bit concerned about my positive feelings in the classroom, and wasn't sure my refreshed perspective was there to stay. It was almost as if I was waiting for the bubble to burst. Not wanting to tempt fate, I banished my self-doubt and focused my energies on my students. As I became more relaxed with them, I found myself having life discussions before class would start, or sometimes, in the middle of a lesson. I hadn't really been in the habit of doing this too much in the past, but now it was happening with greater regularity, and I could feel the kids responding as I shared my experiences with them. Despite the feeling that the kids were listening attentively, I didn't really know if my ramblings were having any impact. I wouldn't have to wait long to find out.

One day, late in February, I received an e-mail from Lynn Marie Fry, mother to Brooke in my first period Civics class. It was a request for work as Brooke was ill and house-bound for a week. I responded, and agreed to meet Brooke's mom to give her some work so Brooke wouldn't fall far behind. Lynn Marie told me that Brooke was very concerned about keeping up with her studies. I well understood as I remembered how my daughter, Dianna, would worry about missing classes due to illness. I smiled at the memory, and wished I had many more students like those two. After meeting Brooke's mom, I was surprised to receive a very warm response by e-mail, thanking me for my efforts. I responded, and before I knew it, we had established a friendship that now has widened to include both our families. The point here is that I was getting very positive feedback from a parent about the things that were happening in my classroom — especially with reference to my ramblings about life lessons. As awareness of my impact on these students increased, I gradually felt I was getting closer to wrestling those previously unanswered questions to the ground. I wasn't just getting closer; I was on the very brink.

What Lynn Marie started, Brooke completed. It happened on the day of the final evaluation — final *exam*, in the old terms — for the course. Brooke finished early, submitted her paper, and asked for a piece of lined paper. As I cruised around the room, I noticed that she was writing what looked like a personal letter. As I came closer it seemed to be more like a poem. Brooke is an excellent student, and I was impressed that she might be writing poetry. Great stuff, I thought. I leaned down and asked if I could read it when she was done. She said ok, and I continued on my rounds. Before the period ended, she gave me the page. I found a moment to read it before the class left the room and it was all I could do to control the tears that were welling in my eyes. It was a poem for me. It was about my class. Brooke didn't know it, but her poem gave me the answer to my questions and clarified my quest for the heart of teaching. I'm including the poem here.

Monday Morning

Monday morning
Dark and gray
Sleepy minds
Try to start their day.

Half awake
Walking down the hall
Room 108
Furthest of them all.

Through the door
And to my seat
And there's Mr. F.
Walking to a beat.

A smile on his face
Joy dances in his eyes
Good morning class!

Greeted with groans and sighs.
This doesn't phase him
He knows what to do
I'll teach about life
Things textbooks can't show you.

My eyes become widened
I am now awake
Learning things I need to know
Not just a class I have to take.

Profound insight
Comes from Room 108
Thanks Mr. F…
I think you're great!

— *Brooke Fry* —

I felt like I had been struck by a lightning bolt. I had shared some of the doubts I had been experiencing about the job I was doing in the classroom with Brooke's mom. She told me on several occasions that I was having a greater impact than I realized and that I really should stop doubting myself. Her support as a parent and as a friend, in combination with Brooke's poem enabled me to put my present circumstances into a clearer perspective. The pieces were beginning to fall into place. What a gift!

Throughout my entire career I had doggedly pursued the achievement of excellence in the classroom. That had been my mission — to keep that demon of fear at bay and become the best teacher I could be. Somehow, on a subconscious level, I knew those pursuits were only a part of the heart of teaching that I'd glimpsed down through the years. Those flashes had whetted my appetite; they had become the driving force in a journey that had seemingly become derailed after the lunch club had closed down. Somehow, I knew that I was getting closer and closer to my goal — to fully understand and experience the heart of teaching. As the semester wore on, I found myself greeting my students at the door with a greater depth of caring than I had ever experienced before. I recall one day in particular, when a student walked in and reminded me, with a very wide smile, that the next day was a holiday — a professional development day. The smile came off my face abruptly. He noticed, and asked incredulously,

"What's the matter, sir? Don't you like holidays?"

"Not everyone has a holiday tomorrow," I growled.

Another student chimed in saying, "Gee sir, you may have to come to school tomorrow, but you don't have to teach any lessons, deal with uniforms, lates, or P.A. interruptions!"

Without thinking, I responded, "I'd far rather be here with you guys because I love you."

The class had all been gleefully listening to the exchange and throwing in their own comments, but when my last response registered, they gasped and fell silent. Realizing what I said, I felt myself blushing. I just stood there looking at them, and they held my gaze. After a few moments I told them that it was true. I meant every word. The silence was deafening. There were no silly remarks, just stillness as they held my eyes with their own. They knew I was serious, and when I looked away and began the lesson, the atmosphere was different somehow. For the balance of the semester Room 108B was a different kind of place. Beneath the usual routines, the lessons, the lighter moments, as well as the frustrations, there was a new undercurrent. There was a new bond, once declared, and then lived out in each succeeding day.

In April, I received an e-mail from my former student, Kenneth Tam, who was finishing his undergraduate program at Wilfrid Laurier University and looking forward to beginning work on his Master's degree in History. He wanted to visit and to see my new digs. We set a date, and then I arranged for Brooke to join us. I wanted her to meet Kenneth — who by this time had published the first four novels of his science fiction series — because I had found out that Brooke was in the process of writing a book of her own. I hoped that Kenneth would share his experience of writing with her. They both agreed and the meeting went well. As Brooke left to go home, I realized that my former student had given me a very valuable insight into the art of writing. I felt very fortunate to have participated in the exchange of ideas and experiences. But I didn't know that Kenneth had a surprise for me.

Once we were alone, Kenneth looked me in the eye and said he had a request to make of me. He continued by saying that he and his parents — Iceberg Publishing — wanted me to write a book for them about my philosophy of teaching. My jaw hit the floor. Kenneth smiled and asked if I would do it. I had felt humbled by other experiences in my life, but never before like this. My thoughts flashed back to the exchange I had with his parents at the launch of his first novel — with his dad in particular. I knew they were serious. I was afraid, but I couldn't refuse. We agreed that I would come up with an outline of ideas and send it to them to see if my interpretation of the project meshed with theirs. When that was done, it was clear we were of like mind. You hold the result in your hands right now.

This project, a very personal expression, forced me to put my entire career under a microscope, identify and analyze the strides forward as well as the missteps. It has been nothing short of cathartic as the process allowed me to discover what all the wonderful people, mentioned in my story, had been leading me towards — yes, the heart of teaching.

The flashes are gone — the glimpses into the heart of teaching are no more. They have been eclipsed by the blinding light of realization. For years I have searched, struggled, fallen down until I almost quit. I have to thank Anne, my bride of thirty-three years, who stood by me, believed in me when I was beset with self-doubt, and encouraged me to continue the quest. There are no adequate words to express my appreciation. But I can, now, at last, describe my understanding of the heart of teaching.

It is within me.

I saw its flashes and felt its tremors as I grew as a person and as a professional.

It doesn't exclude or eclipse the skills one utilizes in the classroom; it is the heart that brings all these things together, forming a power so awesome that it can touch the hearts and souls of my students.

The heart of teaching cannot be acquired, nor can it be learned. It must be lived and it must be shared.

Now it is clear. Now I understand.

Conclusion

Looking back over the years, I recognize that the quest that consumed me throughout my career manifested itself during my childhood and teen years. I can see it in the motives I had for entering this profession. I can see it in the young child and teen experiencing great pleasure in helping others whether they were family, friends, neighbours, or a little boy trapped in a telephone booth. The quest was there even though I didn't know what it was. Internal demons, character flaws, and mistakes made throughout the journey, were all an integral part of the growth process. That young teen struggled his way into early adulthood, experienced failure and took another risk by entering the teaching profession. Circumstances over which he had little control brought him face to face with his demon within. Somehow he found the courage to confront that demon and engage in a battle that lasted for decades.

It is ironic that a professional achievement like the publication of a book for student use distracted me from my path to the point where I became lost. For a short while, the job revolved around me instead of the students in front of me. But I was never alone. So many loving and strong people walked with me, and carried me when I stumbled, nurtured me when I weakened, inspired me when I despaired, and lovingly affirmed me when I doubted. Their support over these years has given me the chance to recognize the responsibility that comes with teaching, and the daunting power it has. I know this power, now, and I am forever humbled by it.

The power can comfort, lead, teach, and inspire, but it can easily be turned to cause hurt, to discourage, and to disappoint. Recognizing this has woken me to a sobering reality — but to an exciting one too. I've realized that I need only be myself —and true to myself — to help my students. I am not a master teacher. I have made many mistakes in the past, and I expect to make more. But I will doubt myself less than in the past. My classroom will never be the same because, for me, the act of the heart of teaching will not be accidental; rather, it will be intentional and focused. I know that I love my students — not because they are brilliant, or beautiful, or responsible, but because they, as wonderful individuals, are their parents' gift to me. Gifts to be loved, nurtured, and inspired. I will always be honest with them.

I have been very blessed throughout my career. Probably the greatest of these blessings is the fact that I have been well-schooled by my students. I wish I could say that I was a quick study. It took a long time for me to approach discipline in a kind and caring way. As a rookie, I fell into the trap of trying to be a 'buddy' in the classroom; then I rebounded to a stricter, more controlling tack. Neither approach works well because each student is a unique individual with his or her own feelings, anxieties, hopes, and dreams. Kids don't need teacher buddies any more than they need to be controlled. Inappropriate student behaviour is not a horrid situation — it is really an opportunity to guide, nurture, and inspire. Despite the fact that I believe this to be true, I still fall flat on my face at times and lash out in anger and frustration. I need to forgive myself at such times. But more importantly, I need to apologize after these incidents — publicly. That is a lesson students will catch.

Just recently, I experienced another episode of anger when several students waltzed into my Civics class late and then others were chatting as I led the class in an opening prayer. I wanted to blow sky high. I wanted to throw something. But I just glared at them and growled something unintelligible instead. They became very, very quiet and stayed that way as I taught the lesson. No fooling around, no friendly banter, just business. After class I felt pretty lousy about things. A couple of my Civics students were next door in their History class during the next period. It was my preparation time so I wandered into that room as I noticed the class was busy doing group work. I chatted for a few moments with the teacher, and then I sat down beside one of the girls who had wandered in late the previous period. She looked uneasily at me and asked how I was.

"I'm not feeling very good," I replied. "As a matter of fact I'm not proud of my reaction last period."

She looked very surprised. I think she had expected a good tongue-lashing.

"I'm sorry I was late for class, sir... there is no excuse."

She continued, "And there was no excuse for our behaviour during prayer either."

"Ok, I guess we just had a bad day together," I responded. I smiled at her and left the room. The next day I apologized to the class for my unfriendly behaviour, and we just moved on. I knew they forgave me, I could see it in their eyes. And they knew I had forgiven them.

Honesty is an important lesson my students have taught me many times over. It's really ok not knowing an answer, or making a spelling error during a lesson. Posturing as the know-all professional is pretentious and it doesn't fool the kids. They want their teachers to be real to them. If I cannot be myself, with all of my warts and wrinkles, I cannot help them, teach them, nor hope to inspire them. I am the adult in the classroom. I'm much more than a tutor or an academic role model, I'm someone who can influence students in a powerful way, and show them how to operate as real and caring human beings. Writing essays, passing tests, and earning credits are all important things in their own right. Teaching lessons is terribly important too. But at the end of the day, the most important thing is the living we do.

Since we teachers are very human, many of us are plagued with inner demons of one kind or another. These fears and anxieties within are not rational, but they are very real; and they prey on our tranquility and self worth. Their goal is very simply to control us. I have battled my own demons for several decades, and I'm sure the battle will continue for the rest of my life. This inner struggle is not easy, but it is winnable. My dad once told me that perfection is not about being flawless or avoiding mistakes, it is about making wrong turns, falling flat on your face, then dusting yourself off and trying again. It is really about the struggle and the will to persevere. By being a real person in the eyes of my students, I will show them that they can do that too.

When a woman or a man steps inside a classroom, the struggle is neither with the students nor the countless interruptions that occur with nerve-wracking regularity. It is within that teacher. It is the struggle to be respectful and loving, and most importantly, to be honest with herself or himself, and with the students.

Honesty, respect and love: these are the truths at the heart of teaching.

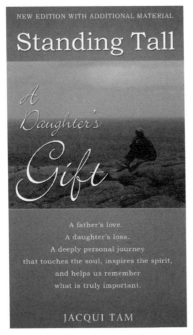

Standing Tall:
A Daughter's Gift

by Jacqui Tam

Standing Tall: A Daughter's Gift is a deeply personal, spiritually-healing memoir written by a daughter in honour of her father. Carrying readers through both the tragedy of Alzheimer's disease and the joys of a remarkable father-daughter relationship... it is touching and enlightening, proving the strength of the human spirit and the immortality of human love. A tribute and a journey, ***A Daughter's Gift*** is a book that reaches the soul... and strengthens it.

www.icebergpublishing.com

THE EQUATIONS NOVELS

The Earthers evolved after humans were driven from the Earth by an intelligent bio-weapon dubbed 'Omega'. They are faster, stronger, smarter, wiser, *better* than humans, and they are the only hope for the survivors of the human race as an interstellar war between two great alien powers absorbs the galaxy. But all is not as it seems, and the humans and the Earthers face challenges that overshadow the wars of alien empires and threaten to destroy their civilizations...

The Equations Novels by Kenneth Tam
   Book One: THE HUMAN EQUATION (Oct 2003)
   Book Two: THE ALIEN EQUATION (May 2004)
   Book Three: THE RENEGADE EQUATION (Dec 2004)
   Book Four: THE EARTHER EQUATION (July 2005)
   Book Five: THE GENESIS EQUATION (July 2006)
   Book Six: THE VENGEANCE EQUATION (July 2007)
   Book Seven: THE NEMESIS EQUATION (July 2008)
   Book Eight: THE DESTINY EQUATION (Forthcoming)

THE CAMPAIGN EQUATION Spin-off Series
   Book One: RETALIATION by Wesley Prewer (July 2006)
   Book Two: PATHFINDERS by Wesley Prewer (Forthcoming)

THE GENESIS SAGA Spin-off Series by John Fioravanti
   Book One: PASSION & STRUGGLE (Forthcoming)

www.earther.net

About the Author

John Fioravanti is a veteran secondary school educator about to complete his thirty-fourth year in the classroom. His teaching career with the Waterloo Catholic District School Board in Ontario has been evenly divided between two schools: St. Benedict in Cambridge, and St. David in Waterloo. He graduated from the History program at St. Jerome's College, University of Waterloo in 1972.

Throughout his career, John has focused on developing research, analysis, and essay writing skills in his History classroom. This led to the publication of his first non-fiction work for student use, *Getting It Right In History Class* (Data Based Directions, 2002), along with an American version of the same title. *A Personal Journey To The Heart Of Teaching* is his second non-fiction work; it attempts to crystallize the struggles, accomplishments, and setbacks experienced in more than three decades of effort to achieve excellence in his chosen field.

John presently lives in Waterloo, Ontario with Anne (his bride of thirty-four years) and their two dogs Buffy and Morley. When he's not renovating and maintaining his house, he's devouring novels of all genres. His children, Dianna, Daniel, and Dominic are threatening to bury him with his favourite novels.